REVOLUTIONARY RED TRACTORS

Lee Klancher & Katie Free

OCTANE PRESS

Octane Press, Edition 1.0, October 2022

Copyright © 2022 by Lee Klancher and Katie Free

On the cover: 1971 Farmall 826. *Lee Klancher*
On the end papers: Farmall M. *Lee Klancher*; Case IH 500. *Lee Klancher*
On the frontispiece: 1954 J. I. Case SC. *Lee Klancher*
On the title page: 1975 rendering of futuristic combine. *Designed by Gregg Montgomery, Montgomery Design International*
On the verso page: Case IH 470 Quadtrac. *Case IH*
On the contents page: 1984 International 7488. *Lee Klancher*
On the back cover: International 1568. *Lee Klancher*

All rights reserved. With the exception of quoting brief passages for the purposes of review, no part of this publication may be reproduced without prior written permission from the publisher.

ISBN: 978-1-64234-123-2
ePub ISBN: 978-1-64234-124-9

LCCN: 2022907799

Edited by Catherine Mandel
Design by Tim Palin Creative
Copyedited by Faith Garcia
Educational Advisor Anita Greenberg, PhD

OCTANE PRESS

octanepress.com

Octane Press is based in Austin, Texas

Printed in China

CONTENTS

CHAPTER 1 | 1830–1905   **EARLY FARM MACHINES** 1

CHAPTER 2 | 1906–1923   **STEP ON THE GAS** 29

CHAPTER 3 | 1924–1956   **TRACTOR TAKEOVER** 59

CHAPTER 4 | 1957–1978   **HORSEPOWER WARS** 91

CHAPTER 5 | 1979–1999   **THE FEW FEED THE MANY** 121

CHAPTER 6 | 2000–2020 AND BEYOND   **COMPUTERS TRANSFORM FARMING** 151

GLOSSARY 180

INDEX 182

Threshermen work on the year's harvest. The belt that runs from the steam engine to the thresher provides the power. It moves when the green wheel turns, like a bicycle chain. *Case IH*

CHAPTER 1 | 1830–1905

EARLY FARM MACHINES

Ten-year-old William Howard has a busy day ahead of him. Instead of walking to school for his lessons, he'll stay home. He needs to help his family on the farm! In the morning, he'll milk the cows. After that, he'll help his father and older brother harvest the wheat.

But William is sick of the constant chores. He doesn't want to spend the day doing the mindless, tiring work of harvesting. He scampers off to the creek with his sister, Mary, to skip rocks and play games. Maybe if their parents don't see them, they'll get to play all day!

Wisconsin Historical Society 24812

It is 1830 and William's family lives on a farm in Ohio. Farming is a family business where everyone pitches in. William is one of eight children. The younger ones take care of the chickens and gather eggs. They also work in the vegetable garden. Older boys like William usually help with the cows and farming. Older girls like Mary often help cook, sew, and wash laundry.

FARMING THROUGH THE AGES

Rogers Fund, 1930, Metropolitan Museum of Art 30.4.2

5000 BCE — Ancient Egyptian farmers use a sickle to cut crops and a **flail** to separate grains.

300 BCE — Chinese farmers use heavy metal plows that cut and turn soil.

Lorraine Keuhnel

1793 — Eli Whitney invents the cotton gin, which removes seeds from cotton.

1834 — Cyrus McCormick patents a reaper that cuts grain.

1836 — Hiram Moore invents the first working combine harvester.

National Museum of American History 2003-35624

1837 — John Deere makes the first self-cleaning plow.

Wisconsin Historical Society 97242

1842 — Jerome Increase Case (J. I. Case) starts the Racine Threshing Machine Works in Racine, Wisconsin.

Case IH

1849 — A. M. Archambault & Company builds the first farm steam engine.

1869 — J. I. Case and Company makes the first steam engine tractor, "Old No. 1"

1876 — J. I. Case builds the first self-propelled traction steam engine.

US Patent US134476A

1884 — Combine harvesters become more popular.

1904 — J. I. Case builds the 150 HP steam tractor.

At the time, horses and other **draft animals** were the main source of **power** on the farm. Their biggest job was pulling heavy **plows**, to break up the soil. That made it easier to plant the seeds that grow into crops. Farmers often kept an extra horse just for this job. But that meant they had to grow even more crops to feed the horses. Each horse needed at least five acres worth of grain. Those extra acres could've been used to grow **cash crops**.

With machines, farmers like the Howards could grow more food with fewer people. Some people moved to cities for work. In 1850, almost 65 percent of all Americans worked in farming. By 1900, that number dropped to 40 percent. Kids still helped, but they weren't quite as necessary for the farm's survival. They could spend more time playing and studying at school.

Three girls play with three baby goats (kid goats). Children often helped raise animals on the farm. *Wisconsin Historical Society 103291*

1831 REAP WHAT YOU SOW

It's fall, the busiest time of the year for the Howard family. The wheat has grown tall, and it must be harvested! But the Howards only have two weeks to reap—or cut and gather—all the wheat before it rots. Every farm in the area is in the same position, so there aren't extra workers to help.

To harvest the wheat, William's father cuts the stalks with a **grain cradle**. He then drops the wheat stalks into neat rows. William's job is to follow his father and tie the grain together into bundles. The work is slow. Their family finishes two acres in one day.

Reaping was often the step that slowed farmers down. They would plant more grain if they could harvest it before it went bad. But farmers often planted fewer acres than they owned to make sure they could reap the entire crop.

Then came a man named Cyrus McCormick. Growing up on his family's farm, he often worked in his family's blacksmith shop, making different inventions. His father had been trying to make a horse-drawn reaping machine that could cut the grain. But he gave up. Cyrus continued the project with his family's slave, Jo Anderson. The two began in the fall of 1831 and finished the machine before the fall harvest was even over. McCormick showed it off to local farmers, but they were not impressed by its funny look and loud clatter.

Despite the lack of interest, McCormick continued to work on his invention. He didn't sell a single machine for nine years! Finally, the reaper began to grow in popularity. In 1847, he and his brother moved to Chicago to start the McCormick Harvesting Machine Company that would manufacture the harvesters. By 1856, McCormick was selling thousands of machines each year.

This painting by N.C. Wyeth depicts what the first demonstration of the reaper might have looked like. Jo Anderson sweeps cut grain off the reaper's platform as Cyrus McCormick walks behind.
Wisconsin Historical Society 4393

FARM FACT

Jo Anderson was a slave on the McCormick plantation. He worked closely with Cyrus McCormick on the reaper but received no credit for his work. Why was Jo Anderson treated so unfairly?

As terrible as it sounds, the government didn't count Black slaves as US citizens. They didn't have the right to claim ownership of an invention. The glory and the money went to McCormick instead of Anderson. Anderson remained a slave until he was freed around the time of the Civil War.

Finally, a law in 1870 gave all Americans—regardless of race or gender— the right to their own inventions.

After hearing about this machine, William's father buys a reaper to help with the harvest. He pays $125, or about $4,500 in today's money. As their horse pulls the reaper, it mows over the grain, cuts the stalks, and pushes them onto a platform. William and his father walk next to the machine and rake the wheat stalks off the platform and onto the ground. Then they tie the piles into neat bundles by hand. Remember how the Howard family could only reap two acres a day with a grain cradle? With the McCormick reaper, they can harvest 10 acres of wheat in a day— five times as much! William's family grows even more wheat, sells it, and makes more money.

A farmer uses a grain cradle to harvest his crop. If he's skilled enough, he'll cut two acres in a day. *Wisconsin Historical Society 67156*

Farmers use a McCormick reaper to cut wheat and rake it into piles. Two workers follow the reaper to bundle the grain. *Case IH*

McCORMICK REAPER

FUN FACT

Many people claim to have invented the reaper. They battled for the title in the mid- and late 1800s. Cyrus McCormick was the first to build and sell a reaper in large quantities, and he is now recognized as the inventor. Many inventions are like this, with several innovators creating similar machines at around the same time. Sometimes only history, popularity, and successful sales can determine who is recognized as the inventor!

PLATFORM
The cut stalks glide across the platform and onto the ground where a farmer can rake them into a bundle.

BLADES
Moving teeth that slice the stalks.

Width: 7 feet

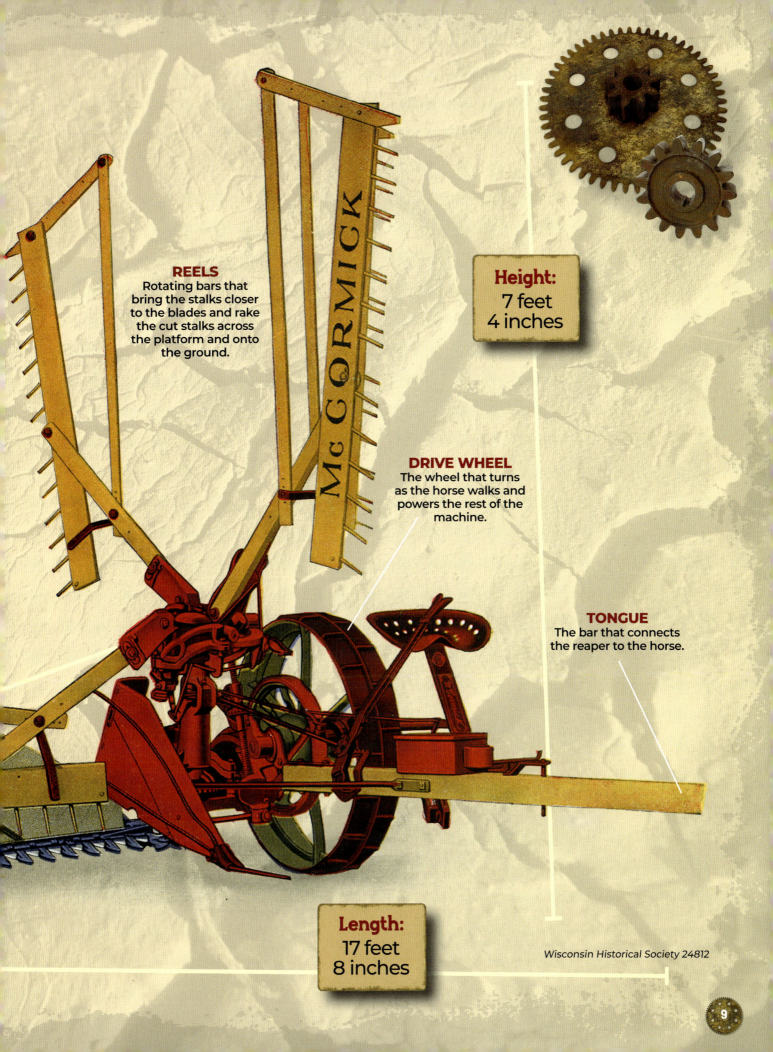

REELS
Rotating bars that bring the stalks closer to the blades and rake the cut stalks across the platform and onto the ground.

Height:
7 feet 4 inches

DRIVE WHEEL
The wheel that turns as the horse walks and powers the rest of the machine.

TONGUE
The bar that connects the reaper to the horse.

Length:
17 feet 8 inches

Wisconsin Historical Society 24812

A man demonstrates the J. I. Case Old No. 1 steam engine to a large crowd. *Case IH*

But this year is different. Instead of horses, a steam engine will power the threshing machine. Henry can't wait to see it! He's heard that they are very loud. The neighboring families have been talking about the steam engine's arrival for weeks.

This steam engine is called "Old No. 1" and was invented by a man named Jerome Increase Case. J. I. Case was born in the state of New York but left for Wisconsin to become a thresherman. He started building threshing machines that were powered by teams of horses. But then, in 1869, Case built an 8-horsepower steam engine that could be pulled from farm to farm by horses. The smoke stack folded down and had a seat where the driver sat and controlled a team of horses. Old No. 1 paved the way for other machines on the farm.

HOW A STEAM ENGINE WORKS

Steam engines were used in many different machines, such as water pumps, trains, and threshers. Here's how they work.

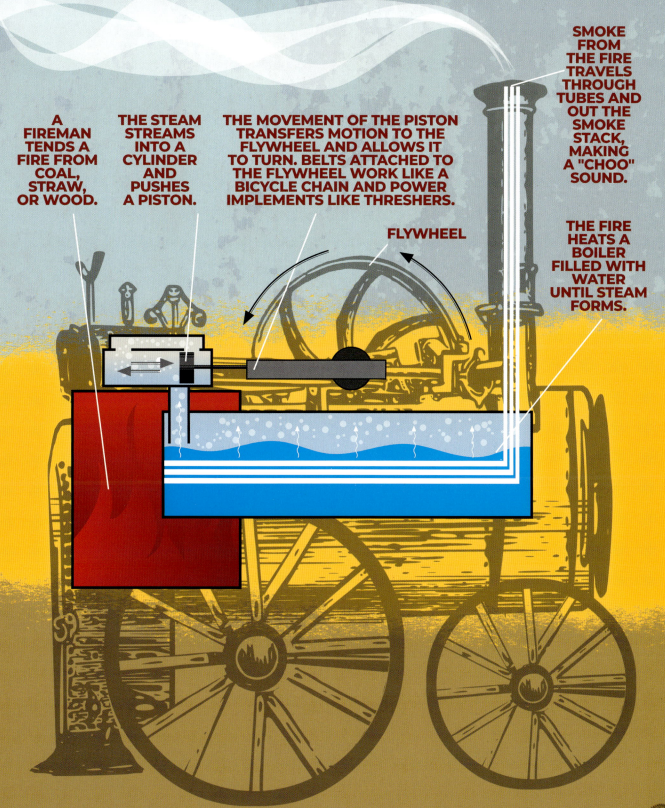

A FIREMAN TENDS A FIRE FROM COAL, STRAW, OR WOOD.

THE STEAM STREAMS INTO A CYLINDER AND PUSHES A PISTON.

THE MOVEMENT OF THE PISTON TRANSFERS MOTION TO THE FLYWHEEL AND ALLOWS IT TO TURN. BELTS ATTACHED TO THE FLYWHEEL WORK LIKE A BICYCLE CHAIN AND POWER IMPLEMENTS LIKE THRESHERS.

SMOKE FROM THE FIRE TRAVELS THROUGH TUBES AND OUT THE SMOKE STACK, MAKING A "CHOO" SOUND.

THE FIRE HEATS A BOILER FILLED WITH WATER UNTIL STEAM FORMS.

FLYWHEEL

Horsepower: 8 horsepower

Top Speed: A team of strong horses can pull this steam engine at 2–3 miles per hour.

Weight: Very heavy! A draft horse can pull 1.5 times its weight if the load is on wheels!

Size: A very similar machine—1857 Lane & Dyer steam engine—was 10 feet 9 inches long, 10 feet high, and 6 feet 6 inches wide.

Case IH

1869 J. I. CASE "OLD NO. 1"

FUN FACT

The "Old No. 1" was J. I. Case's first portable steam engine and was introduced in 1869. It was meant to be pulled by horses. The smokestack folded down and had a seat for the driver. Less than 10 years after introducing the Old No. 1 steam engine, J. I. Case became the most successful maker of farming steam engines in the world.

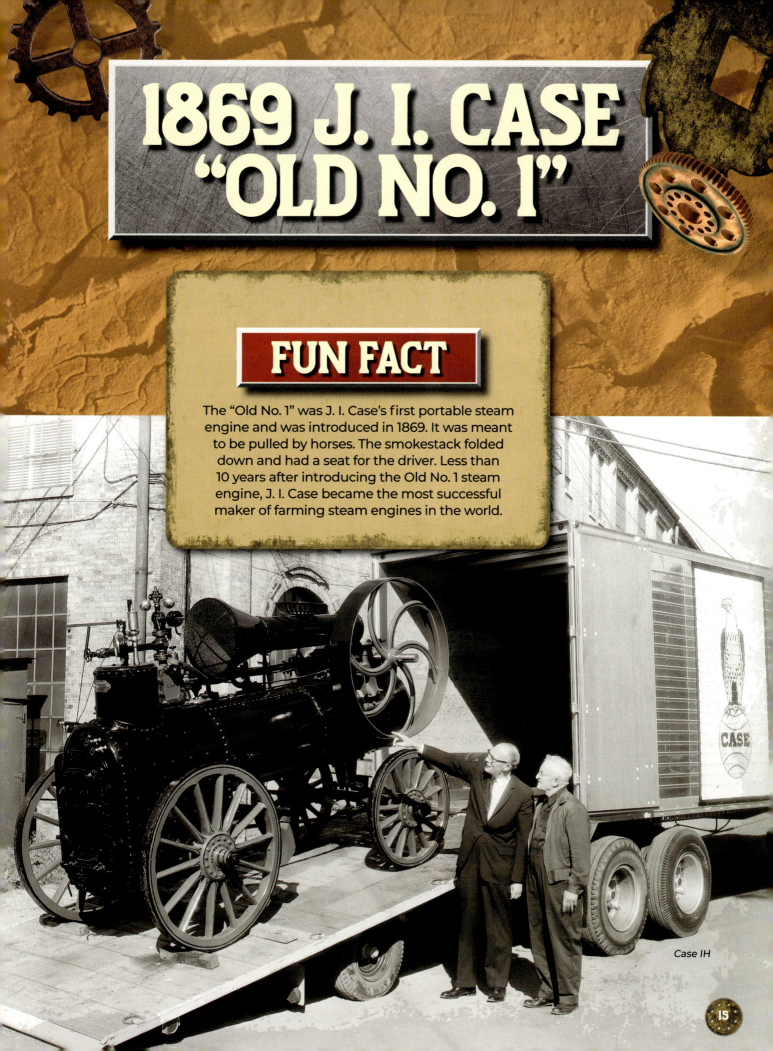

Case IH

1884 THE COMBINE

The McCormick reaper helped farmers. But there were still problems with them. The reaper left piles of wheat, and men like Henry Howard spent an entire day tying up bundles of grain.

Henry Howard has grown up and now has a family and a farm. He has all daughters. Anna, his 12-year-old daughter, helps her father with the harvest. She drives the McCormick reaper, making sure the horse walks in a straight, steady line. Anna's father and his farmhand tie the wheat stalks. By the end of the day, they'll have harvested 10 acres of wheat. But the harvest takes a toll on the men's hands. They're raw and bleeding from the work.

Thankfully, an invention comes along that helps the farming families . . . and their hands! The wire binder cuts and ties bundles of wheat. The Howards' neighbor drops in to show off the new machine. But he later regrets it. His best milking cow dies! It had eaten pieces of metal wire that fell into the grain. Other farmers around the country stumbled across dead livestock that had eaten grain harvested with a wire binder. Anna's father buys a different machine, the Deering twine binder. This binder cuts and bundles wheat with twine, which is harmless to animals.

A four-man crew rides on a combine. The combine can cut 40 acres a day and thresh about 100 bushels an hour. *Library of Congress LC-USZ62-39863*

Anna's father hears that there are large valleys in California that have rich land for farming. The Howards pack up and move farther west. There, Anna sees an invention that blows the binders and reapers away. The combine harvester, or "combine" for short, performs three steps in one. It can reap, thresh, and **winnow** grain.

The first combines were developed on and off through the years. Hiram Moore built the first working combine in Michigan in the 1830s. This machine cut the stalks and pushed the grain into a tube that threshed it. Screens and a fan winnowed the threshed grain by blowing away the **chaff**.

Teams of mules, horses, or even oxen pulled the first combines. Up to 30 mules or horses were needed to pull these giants. Later, combines were steam propelled. Some of them were 18 feet wide!

For some reason, combines were not popular in the Midwest. Instead, farmers relied on machines like reapers, binders, and threshers. More farmers used combines in California. As people flocked to the new state, they began growing wheat and fruit. But there weren't enough workers to harvest the crops, so farmers invented tools to help them. A threshing crew might need 20 to 30 workers. But four or five men could run a combine. The combine **revolutionized** agriculture.

A farmer drives a horse-drawn McCormick grain binder. Grain binders saved time and labor during the reaping process.
Wisconsin Historical Society 57797

An ad promotes the Deering binder. This new machine saved people's hands and backs from the difficult task of bundling grain. *Wisconsin Historical Society 57797*

UNITS OF MEASUREMENT

ACRES

Farms are usually measured in acres. An acre can be any shape. One acre is equal to 43,560 square feet, or 0.404 hectares. A football field is 57,600 square feet (360 feet long x 160 feet wide). A football field is 1.32 acres!

57,600 SQUARE FEET

43,560 SQUARE FEET

BUSHELS

Farmers often sell their crops in bushels. But how much is a bushel? It is a big amount, but one that you could probably carry for a short distance. Here are some examples of what makes up a bushel.

1 BUSHEL = 8 GALLONS OF MILK OR 56 POUNDS OF CORN OR 60 POUNDS OF WHEAT OR 125 APPLES

HORSEPOWER

Ever wondered what horsepower is? It's the unit of power needed to lift 550 pounds at a rate of 1 foot per second. James Watt, a Scottish engineer, wanted to compare a horse's strength to his newly built steam engine. The idea was that an 8-horsepower machine was as powerful as eight horses. But because some horses are more powerful than others, it was impossible to calculate the power of one horse, and Watts overestimated a horse's strength. Nevertheless, the term is here to stay!

Early gas tractors were known by two horsepower ratings: belt and drawbar. These were the two ways the machine worked. Drawbar power involved pulling an implement like a plow over the ground. Tractors used belt power to run stationary machines, such as threshers. Drawbar power was usually about half of the belt power. That's because it took a lot of energy to just drive over the ground. A Titan 10-20 had a rating of 10 horsepower for jobs like plowing, and 20 horsepower for jobs like threshing.

Do you have any pets? Could you set up the same system that James Watt set up but figure out dogpower, catpower, turtlepower? How about hamsterpower or fishpower? Can you draw what a contraption like that would look like?

1 HORSEPOWER = 33,000 LBS / PER FOOT / MIN

420 HORSEPOWER/ 0–60 IN 4.7 SECONDS

1915 McCORMICK NO. 1 HARVESTER-THRESHER

The wheat was cut with blades and pushed onto a platform with reels just like the reaper.

A vibrating conveyor belt carried the wheat from the platform and into the machine's body.

FUN FACT

The McCormick No. 1 Harvester-Thresher was designed from 1910 to 1913 and was released to farmers in 1915. It was the first of its kind at the company. By March 1919, it began calling its harvester-threshers "combines."

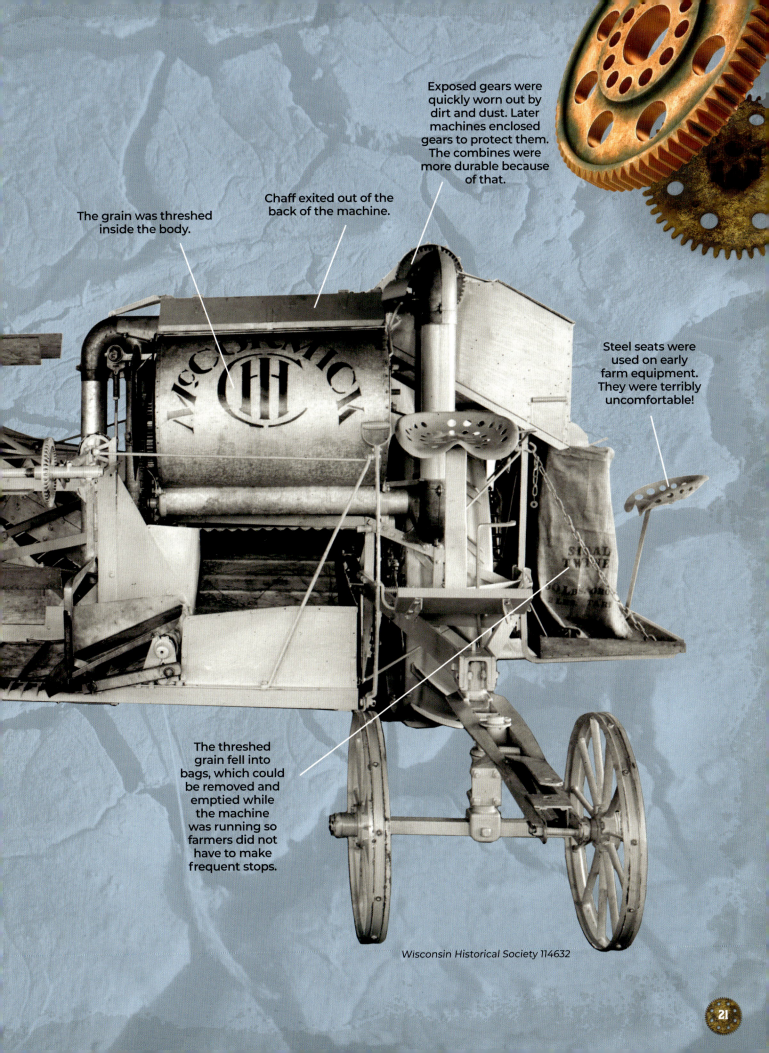

Wisconsin Historical Society 114632

1904 | STEAM GIANT

Anna Howard enjoys working on her family farm in California. But she misses the vast fields of the Great Plains. So, when she is old enough, she applies for a homestead. Her father rails against the idea because he wants her to stay close to home. But Anna is ready for her own homestead. She packs up and moves near her cousins in Nebraska.

Anna's land has never been plowed before. She struggles to break up the dirt with horse-pulled plows. The land is nice and flat, but the soil is hard. After all, it had been buffalo grassland for a long time! But thankfully, there's a machine that can pull the plows: the self-propelled steam tractor.

Only nine Case 150 HPs were ever built. They were sold to mining, lumber, and grain companies to haul heavy loads. Engineer Kory Anderson built this replica in 2018. *Kory Anderson*

In 1876, Case built its first self-propelled **traction engine**, or steam-powered tractor. Steam-powered tractors weren't a common sight in the 1800s, but as the century ended, they became more popular.

These giant machines plodded along at a speed of 2 to 3 miles per hour. They attached to rows of plows called **gangplows**. Even though they could move on their own, teams of horses steered them. Many weighed more than 20 tons! The massive tractors often got stuck in plowed or muddy fields. But they were well-suited for the hard and flat prairie ground.

Anna can't afford to buy a steam tractor, but she can rent one. These tractors need engineers to operate them. And a team must manage the horses that steer the tractors. It is not cheap to have that help. But the price is worth it because a steam-powered tractor can plow up to 75 acres a day.

Eventually, Anna marries and has children. Her 10-year-old son, George, loves watching the chugging steam tractors in action. He hopes to be an engineer someday and drive an engine. His favorite engine is the colossal Case 150 HP. It was the largest steam tractor ever built and weighed about 75,000 pounds! Designed for hauling massive loads over far distances, only nine of them were made.

By 1900, companies were building about 5,000 large steam traction engines per year. But as incredible as these machines were, there were many drawbacks to steam power. These engines puffed out smelly black smoke, and their loud clanging startled the horses. Sometimes sparks flew out of the engines and set the grass or straw on fire. Occasionally, the steam engines even blew up! Explosions were common in the early 1900s—about two a day. The main source of power on farms was still horses. Steam power couldn't replace reliable, safe draft animals!

Two men stand next to the Case 150 HP, the largest steam tractor ever built. *Case IH*

This ad was created to promote Case steam tractors. Between 1869 and 1924 Case sold about 36,000 steam engines. *Case IH*

One day, as the Howards are eating lunch, they hear a thundering boom, and the sky turns black. They hurry toward the bang to their neighbor's farm. The steam engine that had been plowing the fields exploded! The engineer hadn't been watching the boiler closely enough, and the steam had become too powerful to contain. The blast threw the engineer and fireman over 100 feet, killing them on impact.

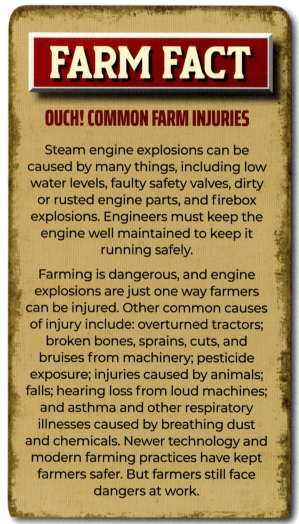

FARM FACT

OUCH! COMMON FARM INJURIES

Steam engine explosions can be caused by many things, including low water levels, faulty safety valves, dirty or rusted engine parts, and firebox explosions. Engineers must keep the engine well maintained to keep it running safely.

Farming is dangerous, and engine explosions are just one way farmers can be injured. Other common causes of injury include: overturned tractors; broken bones, sprains, cuts, and bruises from machinery; pesticide exposure; injuries caused by animals; falls; hearing loss from loud machines; and asthma and other respiratory illnesses caused by breathing dust and chemicals. Newer technology and modern farming practices have kept farmers safer. But farmers still face dangers at work.

REBUILDING THE CASE 150 HP

Kory Anderson was 10 years old when he saw an original boiler from a Case 150 HP steam tractor. After that day, he dreamed about seeing the complete tractor in all its glory. But at age 16, Anderson realized that wouldn't happen unless he built it! He learned the skills he'd need to build a Case 150 HP from scratch. Case sent him the original blueprints, and Anderson made the parts for the tractor. With his friends and mentors, he finished a working replica in 2018. Anderson drove it for the first time in public in Andover, South Dakota. Now, people from all over the world travel to see the Case 150 HP in action!

Kory Anderson

Kory Anderson works on the Case 150 HP. He spent 10 years casting the parts for the steam traction engine. *Kory Anderson*

The Case 150 is so powerful it can pull a gangplow that requires several people to direct the blades while they go for a ride and churn the soil. How many people does it take to run this plow? *Kory Anderson*

Kory Anderson

Width: 14 feet

CASE 150 HP

Horsepower:
150 belt horsepower

Weight:
75,000 pounds

Top Speed:
5.7 miles per hour

Length:
25 feet

Height:
12 feet 6 inches

FUN FACT

Nicknamed the *Titanic* of tractors, the J. I. Case 150 HP was the largest steam tractor ever built! It holds 3 tons of coal and 650 gallons of water! Only a few were built in 1905, but none survive. The example shown here is a replica.

Kory Anderson sits atop the Case 150 HP that he built from scratch.
Kory Anderson

A farmer drives a refurbished International 15-30. Built from 1918 to 1921, the International 15-30 was one of IH's earliest gas tractors. *Lee Klancher*

CHAPTER 2 | 1906–1923

STEP ON THE GAS

In 1923, Edward Brightwell runs toward the tractor in excitement. After supper, his mother had asked, "Edward, why don't you put the tractor away?" Edward is 11 years old and has never driven the tractor. He climbs onto the seat, knowing his whole family is watching him. He pushes the clutch, puts the tractor in gear, and releases the clutch. But instead of moving forward, he lurches backward!

In two seconds, the tractor tears down the barbed wire fence and is lumbering toward the water pump. Thankfully, Edward stops the tractor in time. He moves the gear to

The experimental McCormick Auto-Mower was one of the first gas tractors ever built. *Wisconsin Historical Society 91790*

BY THE NUMBERS

SAVING TIME

The number of bushels farmers could produce with 10 hours of work jumped between 1900 and 1920. Technology was a big reason.

9.26 BUSHELS

9.42 BUSHELS

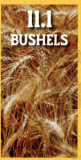
11.1 BUSHELS

1900
TOOLS: STEAM ENGINE, HORSE-PULLED BINDER, AND STEAM-POWERED THRESHER

1910
TOOLS: GAS TRACTOR, HORSE-PULLED BINDER, STEAM-POWERED THRESHER

1920
TOOLS: GAS TRACTOR, TRACTOR-PULLED BINDER, TRACTOR-POWERED THRESHER

Source: Cooper, Barton, and Brodell. Progress of Farm Mechanization. USDA, 1947

A GROWING COUNTRY

The US population soared between 1890 and 1930. What happened to the farm population during that time? How do you think this change affected the rest of the country?

Year	US Population	US Farm Population
1890	64,713,188	9,960,000
1900	78,763,706	11,680,000
1910	95,863,718	11,770,000
1920	111,271,341	10,790,000
1930	128,119,335	8,441,000

Source: https://ourworldindata.org/employment-in-agriculture#number-of-people-working-in-agriculture
Source: https://ourworldindata.org/grapher/population-past-future?tab=chart&country=POL~USA~PRT~PYF

MOVING INTO THE MODERN WORLD

During the 1900s, modern conveniences such as electricity, telephones, and passenger cars became more common.

PERCENTAGE OF AMERICAN HOMES WITH ELECTRICITY

Year	%
1907	8.0%
1912	15.9%
1917	24.3%
1922	40.0%
1927	63.1%

TELEPHONES IN THE US PER 1,000 PEOPLE

Year	Number
1900	17.6
1910	82.0
1920	123.9

CARS SOLD IN THE US EACH YEAR

Year	Number
1900	4,192
1905	24,250
1910	181,000
1915	895,930
1920	1,905,560
1925	3,735,171

Source: https://www.census.gov/library/publications/1960/compendia/hist_stats_colonial-1957.html

An experimental tractor outside Deering Works in 1912. Look at the size of those wheels! *Wisconsin Historical Society 24877*

forward drive and carefully parks the tractor in the shed. Edward hangs his head. It will be a long time before he gets to drive the tractor again!

Twenty-three years earlier, Edward's mother couldn't have imagined driving a tractor. In 1900, farmers had three power sources: their own strength, draft animals, and steam engines. Steam engines helped a lot on the farm, especially when it came to plowing fields and threshing grain. But they were huge, bulky, and hard to use. They also exploded sometimes! Horses and mules were still the main source of power on farms. In 1910, more than 24 million horses and mules lived on American farms. Each farm owned three or four draft animals.

The next 20 years would see huge changes, both on the farm and in the cities. In cities, many houses had indoor plumbing and electricity. Many homes across the US had telephones. With the boom of automobiles, farmers and city folk alike became used to using them as means of transportation..

During this era, many people moved to the cities for jobs and the conveniences of city life. The year 1920 marked the first time where more people lived in cities than the country. To make up for the lost farmhands, tractor power came into play. With the invention of the **internal combustion** engine, tractors became smaller, lighter, and gasoline powered.

Tractors became more common on farms. In 1902, McCormick's company merged with Deering and three other companies to form the International Harvester Company (IH). Suddenly, it was the fourth-largest company in the US! In 1905, there were only six tractor makers in the US. But by 1921, there were 186 companies selling hundreds of different kinds of tractors. The number of tractors on farms approached 200,000. By 1921, almost no one was building steam traction engines.

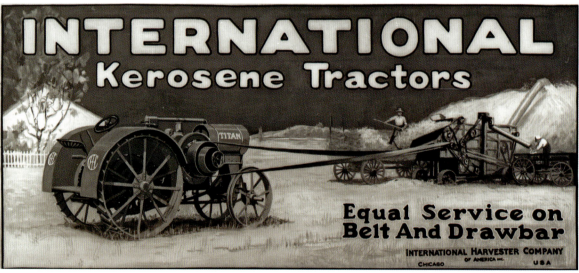

International Harvester Company ran these two ads with one boasting it made one tractor "every 5 minutes." *Wisconsin Historical Society 134627*

FARMING THROUGH THE AGES

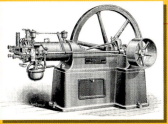

Public Domain, appeared in Popular Science Monthly Volume 18

1872 — Nicholas Otto invents the four-stroke internal combustion engine.

1892 — John Froelich builds the first successful gasoline-powered tractor that can be driven both backward and forward.

1892 — J. I. Case creates and tests a gas tractor but doesn't end up putting it on the market until 1911. Until then, the market for steam was still high.

Case IH

1902 — International Harvester Company (IH) is formed.

1905 — IH builds its first gas-powered tractor, the Friction-Drive tractor.

Library of Congress LC-USZ62-118659

1908 — Ford releases the Model T automobile, selling 15 million during its production run.

1909 — IH premieres the Mogul line of tractors. The Titan line is released a year later.

Case IH

1913 — Sales of steam-powered tractors are at their highest, but gas power will soon overtake steam.

1914 — World War I begins. The US will not enter until 1917. The war ends in 1918.

Library of Congress LC-DIG-ppmsca-51077

1917 — Ford introduces the Fordson, which becomes the most popular tractor in the US.

Library of Congress LC-DIG-npcc-07235

1919 — IH develops the first commercially available power take-off (PTO) system, which debuts in the International 8-16.

1921 — The McCormick-Deering 10-20 premieres.

1906 | FILL 'ER UP!

In 1906, Edward's mother, Clara, is a young girl. Her family hires a steam engine crew to plow the fields. The crew moves down the rows, churning up last year's dried-out crop. Clara watches in horror as a spark falls from the steam engine and lights the dry grass on fire! Thankfully, the crew stops the fire from spreading. Clara overhears them talking about people's farms that had completely burned from a steam engine spark. After that, Clara's father swears that he'll only rent gas-powered tractors.

Two 10-year-old children stand next to an International 8-16 tractor. They are harvesting grain for their grandfather.
Wisconsin Historical Society 8533

Gas-powered engines had many advantages over steam. Compared to coal and wood, gas was easier to use and cheaper to transport. Gas-powered engines only needed a few minutes to start up and they ran all day on a tank of fuel. Plus, they wouldn't light a field on fire!

In 1892, John Froelich invented the first gas-powered tractor that moved backward and forward. He lived in Iowa and owned a threshing service that traveled from farm to farm.

Froelich also liked to tinker with machines. He built a gas-powered tractor that was easier to use than a steam engine. Froelich set off for a nearby field to see if his tractor worked. It fired up and moved at a speed of 3 miles per hour! Over 52 days, the gas tractor threshed 72,000 bushels and only used 26 gallons of gas! Froelich started a company that was eventually bought by John Deere.

The first gas-powered IH tractor to make it to market was built in 1906. The top speed was only 2 miles per hour! The tractor weighed about 13,500 pounds, about the weight of a large African male elephant.

IH continued to make new models of tractors through the early 1910s. The two main lines were the Titan tractors and the Mogul tractors. The first versions of these tractors were

A Titan 45 in a field. Only a handful of these machines survive today.
Lee Klancher

painful to drive. The exhaust pipes blew gas, sand, and grit onto the driver! Later models had longer exhaust pipes and a tin roof to make the driver more comfortable. Engineers were always making changes to improve tractors at IH!

To get an engine started, it must spin fast enough to pump in fuel. It also needs a strong spark. Then the engine can run on its own. If anyone thought a regular car was hard to start, the Titan and Mogul engines felt almost impossible. Clara's neighbor used a horse to start their Titan. They tied a rope around the belt pulley a few times and then attached the other end to the horse. As the horse moved into a trot, it turned the engine enough to fire it up. One time, the tractor fired up and quickly reared backward. It knocked the horse off its feet! After that, the horse stayed far away from tractors.

Early gas tractors were heavy, difficult to operate, and had low horsepower. They often weighed between 20,000 and 30,000 pounds! These early tractors were mostly a replacement for large steam tractors. Clara's family can't afford a large tractor. It doesn't make sense for their small farm. Instead, they keep horses for most jobs and hire tractors for plowing and threshing.

Two farmers pose with their Mogul 45. Look at the size of the wheels!
Minnesota Historical Society

THE INTERNAL COMBUSTION ENGINE

Unlike steam engines, which have a large fire inside a metal box that heats water to create steam pressure in a chamber, internal combustion engines are powered by many small explosions that take place inside the engine. **Pistons** move up and down inside tubes called **cylinders**. The pistons transform the tiny explosions (heat energy) into mechanical power. The pistons' movements spin the engine's **crankshaft**, like a bicycle pedal. The spinning of the crankshaft powers the drive wheels.

Here are the four steps, or strokes, of a gasoline internal combustion engine:

STEP 1: INTAKE

The intake valves open. The piston moves down and draws in a mixture of gas and air. Gas will not ignite unless it's mixed with air.

STEP 2: COMPRESSION

The intake valves close and the piston moves up, compressing—or pressing on—the air.

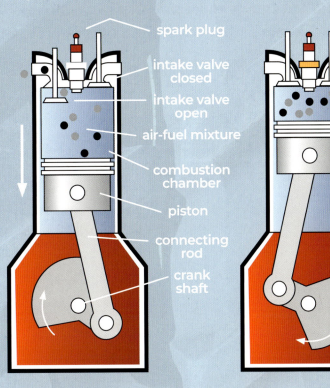

spark plug
intake valve closed
intake valve open
air-fuel mixture
combustion chamber
piston
connecting rod
crank shaft

STEP 3: POWER

Boom! A spark plug lights the gas-air mixture. This makes hot gases that expand and push the piston down. This step gets the wheels moving.

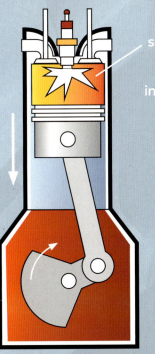

spark plug firing
intake valve open

STEP 4: EXHAUST

As the piston moves up, **exhaust** valves open to let out gases. Then the valves close and the process starts over again.

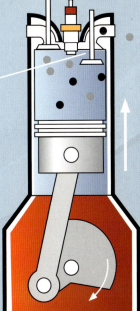

Source: https://www.britannica.com/technology/four-stroke-cycle

FUN FACT

This tractor was IH's first gas tractor! They were initially offered in 20- or 25-horsepower models, and later models included 8- and 12-horsepower options. IH built the Friction-Drive tractor by adding one of its engines to another company's frame.

Height: 9 feet

Width: 8 feet 2 inches

1908 INTERNATIONAL FRICTION-DRIVE TRACTOR

Horsepower: 20 belt horsepower

Weight: 13,000 pounds

Top Speed: 2.0 miles per hour

Length: 14 feet 10 inches

Wisconsin Historical Society 70676

1915 | SMALL BUT MIGHTY

Now Clara is a young married woman with a farm of her own and two-year-old Edward. She has engines that pump water and churn butter. These machines save tons of time! She and her husband talk about buying a tractor to help with the crops. But many neighbors laugh at the idea. Early tractors were crude machines. The parts were open to the air and needed to be constantly cleaned of dust and dirt. They were unreliable and loud. A team of horses could do a better job!

But as the years moved along, tractors became smaller and cheaper. IH began experimenting and building smaller tractors. In the mid- to late 1910s, dozens of tractor companies popped up. By 1916, almost 100 manufacturers sold tractors.

A man plows with his Mogul 8-16 tractor. Can you see how the blades are cutting into the soil to plow the fields and make the soil ready for planting? *Wisconsin Historical Society 73569*

One thing that changed the farmers' perspectives was World War I. The war began in 1914 in Europe. Busy fighting, many nations struggled to feed their citizens and soldiers. The US joined the war in 1917. Even before the US entered the war, it had a large effect on farm

A World War I soldier returns home to find a new Titan 10-20 tractor sitting in a field. In 1919, IH sold 17,234 Titan 10-20s. *Wisconsin Historical Society 3557*

tractors. Many of the world's men left the fields to go to battle or to build weapons for the war. Farms couldn't find workers. To keep feeding the US and its Allies, tractors made up for the lost men.

The US encouraged farmers to grow more food and loaned them money to buy more land and tractors. With this extra cash, farmers bought almost 50,000 tractors. Even with fewer acres and a declining farm population, farms grew more and more crops. Tractors were a big reason for that!

IH responded to the interest by building smaller models of their Titan and Mogul tractors: the Titan 15-30, Mogul 8-16, Mogul 10-20, and Titan 10-20. They weighed under 10,000 pounds, cost less, and were more reliable. They could plow and drive **mowers** and reapers.

Clara and her husband buy a tractor after they hear that the Titan 10-20 plowed for 60 hours straight during a demonstration in Carlinfield, Illinois. Soon, a brand-new Titan 10-20 sits in a shed by the barn.

Clara likes machines. She takes care of her new tractor. Like many tractors of the day, the Titan doesn't have a **radiator** to keep the engine cool. Instead, hot water rises from the engine into a water-cooling tank, while the cooler water sinks down toward the engine. Clara replaces the old, piping hot water with cool, fresh water from the pond.

She also fills the grease cups. Oil keeps engine parts **lubricated** and prevents them from rubbing against each other. Instead of having a modern system where a pump moves oil through the engine, oil drips onto parts of the engine to keep everything running smoothly.

The Titan 10-20 was the first great success of the IH tractor line. Between 1916 and 1922, IH built more than 78,000 of these tractors. Soon, they would face fierce competition from an unlikely place.

A father and son sit atop a makeshift tractor they built from an old Buick car. Farmers were the experts about what was needed in the fields. If companies were not able to give them what they needed, farmers could usually figure out how to build it themselves. *Edwin Rosskam / Library of Congress LC-DIG-FSA-8A15039*

CHANGE THE OIL!

Why do we need to change the oil in cars? Clean oil is important for keeping an engine running smoothly. It helps in three main ways:

Reduce Friction

Friction is the force that causes resistance when one object moves over another. Oil reduces friction by helping engine parts move past each other more smoothly. This prevents wear and tear on the engine.

Cool Things Down

Friction creates a lot of heat. You can feel this if you rub your hands together fast. The moving parts of the engine slide against each other and can create a lot of heat. By reducing friction, oil helps cool the engine.

Clean It Out

Burning gas produces soot. Without oil, the soot would gunk up the engine. Oil helps flush it out.

Farmers change used oil out for new, clean oil on a tractor. *Wisconsin Historical Society 25493*

Over time, oil degrades and gets dirty. This dirty oil is less effective at reducing friction and cooling the engine. The solution is to drain out the old oil and put in fresh, new oil. That's why you need to change it!

FARMERETTES: WOMEN IN WWI

Library of Congress 00652171

When millions of American men joined the war effort, women stepped in to replace them in the fields. A group of women in New York formed the Women's Land Army of America, even before women had the right to vote.

Called "farmerettes," these women were trained to grow crops to help feed the nation. Many farmers disliked the idea of women working in the fields. But they soon appreciated the help once the farmerettes were driving tractors, plowing fields, and harvesting crops. Between 15,000 and 20,000 women grew crops for the Women's Land Army during 1918 and 1919, towards the end of World War I.

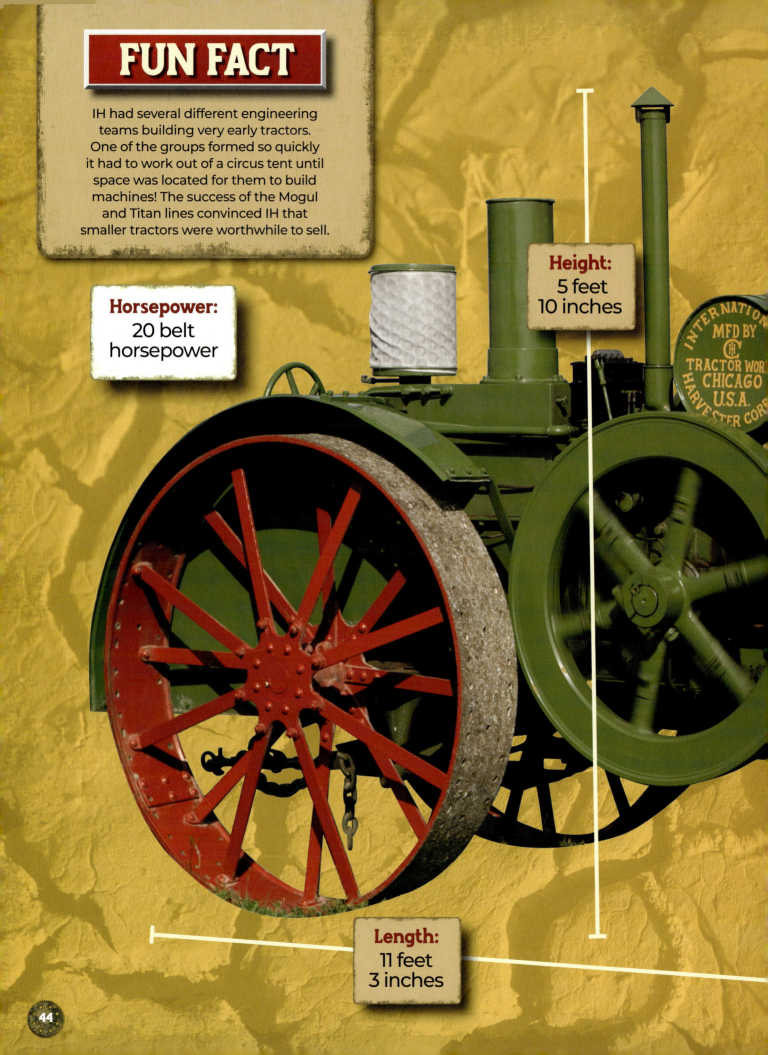

FUN FACT

IH had several different engineering teams building very early tractors. One of the groups formed so quickly it had to work out of a circus tent until space was located for them to build machines! The success of the Mogul and Titan lines convinced IH that smaller tractors were worthwhile to sell.

Horsepower:
20 belt horsepower

Height:
5 feet 10 inches

Length:
11 feet 3 inches

1919 MOGUL 10-20

Weight: 5,500 pounds

Top Speed: 4.0 miles per hour

Width: 4 feet 8 inches

Lee Klancher

As the tractor wars heated up, tractor demonstrations that hyped one brand over another became popular. *Wisconsin Historical Society 46212*

With increased competition against Ford, IH ramped up improvements to the tractor. The company unveiled the International 8-16 in 1917. It was the first IH tractor to be built on an assembly line like the Fordson.

The 8-16 made history by being the first tractor with **power take-off**. This feature allowed implements like plows to be powered by the tractor and not from a wheel rolling on the ground. It allowed for more complex machinery to be attached to tractors and not just stationary engines. Soon, all tractors adopted power take-off.

Unlike IH, Ford didn't work hard to improve the Fordson. Instead, it focused on cars. In 1928, Ford left the US tractor business.

UPS AND DOWNS

World War I lasted from 1914 to 1918. It had a large effect on crop prices.
What trends do you see?
Looking at the graphs, what year were prices the highest?
Why do you think prices were highest at that time?

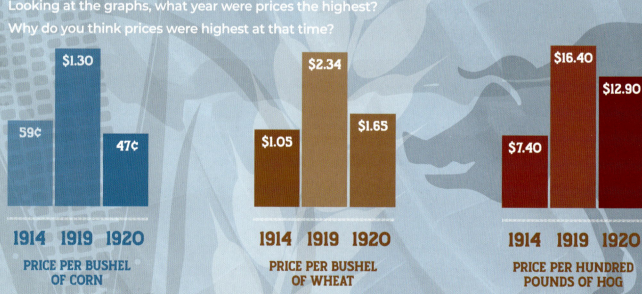

1914	1919	1920
59¢	$1.30	47¢

PRICE PER BUSHEL OF CORN

1914	1919	1920
$1.05	$2.34	$1.65

PRICE PER BUSHEL OF WHEAT

1914	1919	1920
$7.40	$16.40	$12.90

PRICE PER HUNDRED POUNDS OF HOG

Source: https://www.mnopedia.org/agricultural-depression-1920-1934

LINING UP: WHAT IS AN ASSEMBLY LINE?

An assembly line is used to build a product in many small steps.

Assembly lines were popularized in the early part of the twentieth century. Today, they are used to make almost everything, including cars, refrigerators, and candy bars.

Henry Ford didn't invent the assembly line, but he was the first to use it to produce a large number of vehicles. Instead of one person building a car in a single location, an assembly line used a team of people, and each one added a piece to the vehicle as it traveled down the line. Each person was responsible for one step in the process. When it reached the end of the line, most of the parts were in place and the completed vehicle rolled off.

Why was this beneficial?

If one person was building a car, they needed to know everything about every single step, like how to build an engine and wire the lights. Now, a person could do one task quickly and move the rest of the job down the line. That made building a car much faster.

Who in your house is responsible for making dinner? If everyone pitched in could an assembly line for preparing dinner be set up? What would that look like? What part of the process would you like to do?

FUN FACT

The International 8-16 was the first tractor to offer power take-off, a feature that powers tractor tools. It was a big advance in farming! Soon, farmers began hooking up grain binders to the power take-off shafts.

Horsepower: 16.52 belt horsepower

Top Speed: 4.1 miles per hour

Height: 5 feet 5 inches

Width: 4 feet 6 inches

Lee Klancher

1918 INTERNATIONAL 8-16

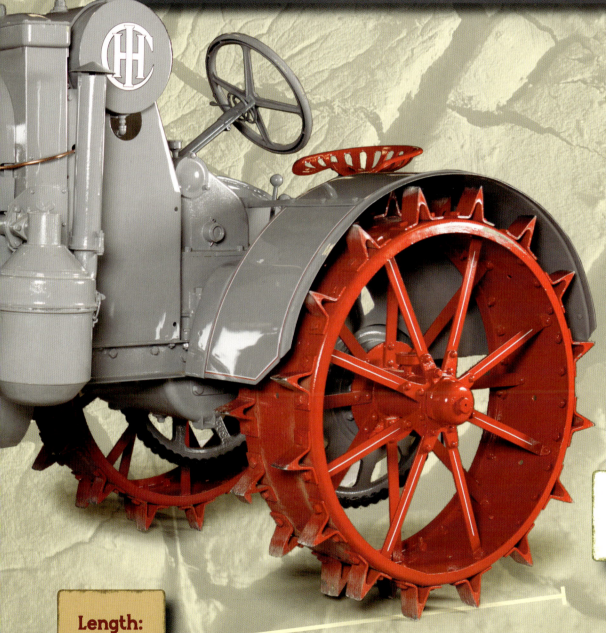

Weight: 3,660 pounds

Length: 11 feet

1923 | POWER CHANGES EVERYTHING

Edward is busy this cold spring morning. Besides his regular chores, he must feed the newborn calves and pigs. It's also time to plow the fields for this year's crop. Part of his job is to keep the Titan 10-20 running. He refills the water tank and adds oil to the grease cups. The engine isn't covered up, so oil splatters everywhere when it runs.

A boy carries a bucket of feed for the pigs. Children often helped around the farm: there was a lot of work to be done and everyone needed to pitch in!
Library of Congress LC-DIG-fsa-8b35241

The Titan is only eight years old, but it feels ancient. During this era, tractors changed so quickly that farmers could only expect five years from their tractors before they became outdated. Edward's parents are already talking about buying a new one.

International 8-16s were used in the price war against Ford. But they couldn't compete against the low-cost Fordson. IH needed another tractor that farmers would choose over the Fordson. In 1921, it had its answer: the McCormick-Deering 10-20 and 15-30. With these models, IH created a rough version of the modern tractor.

The McCormick-Deerings had two main changes from the 8-16s. First, the engine and **transmission** were covered by a frame. This frame kept the engine parts clean and clear from dirt and grime. Early engines were exposed. The moving parts sprayed oil everywhere and made a mess. Also, dirt and dust stuck to moving engine parts, causing wear and tear to the engine. Farmers had to clean these engines constantly to keep them running.

A parade in Chicago celebrates the Boys Working Reserve. Like the Farmerettes, these boys helped grow crops during World War I. *National Archives 20808872*

The 15-30's second key advance was the gear **final drive**. Most of the previous IH tractors used roller chain final drive. Adding a gear final drive made the McCormick-Deerings much easier to maintain than earlier tractors.

Edward's family buys a McCormick-Deering after hearing about these improvements. Compared to their Titan 10-20, it's much easier to drive. Simply turning the steering wheel on the Titan was nearly impossible. But even though McCormick-Deerings have major advancements, they still have their quirks. Their iron wheels make for a bone-shattering ride. The family jokes about how fast their pants wear out. The iron seats and wheels rough them up!

Like the International 8-16, the McCormick-Deering comes equipped with power take-off. Edward's parents warn him about staying away from the shaft when it is spinning. Power take-offs can cause serious injuries to farmers. One of Edward's neighbors lost his arm when his shirt got caught. Thankfully, his wife shut off the tractor before he lost his life too! As a warning, farmers in the area now say, "What the PTO gets, it keeps."

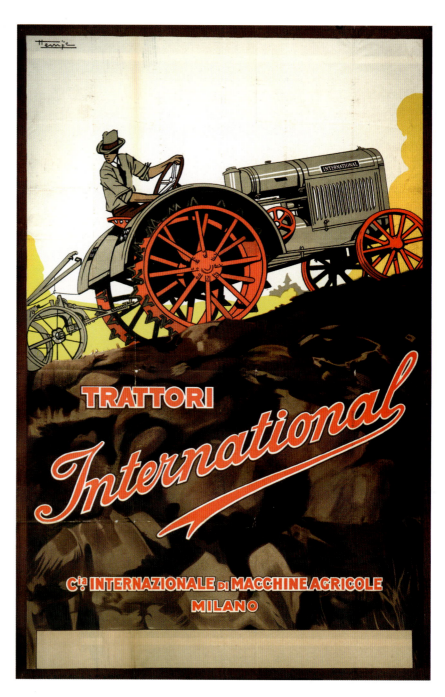

IH machinery wasn't just popular in the US. The company sold tractors all over the world, including Italy. *Wisconsin Historical Society 4255*

TRACTOR TALK

Where Did the Word "Tractor" Come From?

The word "tractor" wasn't new in 1903. But the name became popular after the Hart-Parr Company used it to advertise their machines. The sales manager wanted to combine the words "traction" and "motor" in the ad and wrote "tractor." After that, the name stuck.

The word "tractor" is an example of a portmanteau (a blend of parts of two or more words to make a new word). Can you think of any other portmanteaus used in the English language? Try making a few up!

Cranky!

Early gas-powered vehicles had a crank to get the engine turning enough to start. Often, these cranks could be dangerous. Sometimes the engines would kick backward and break the fingers or arm of the person handling the crank. Sometimes the crank would fly off and hit someone in the head. Worse, if the vehicle wasn't in neutral and if the parking brake was off, it could run over the user when it started.

Hand cranking was the most common cause of injury in the automobile's early days. In fact, the term "cranky" came from the person's mood after starting a car!

Wisconsin Historical Society 53233

NEW DESIGN: THE POWER TAKE-OFF

Belts attached to big wheels were used to power farming implements before the power take-off (PTO) was invented. But a belt on a tractor could only power tools like threshers when it wasn't moving. The PTO changed how farmers used tractors forever. The tractor's motor turns a metal shaft in the PTO. That rotation then powers the tools, whether the tractor is moving or not. The shaft is spinning at an incredibly high rate and can be very dangerous.

Hay balers, woodchippers, harvesters, and mowers are some tools that are driven by the PTO. In this photo, silage (chopped corn) is being blown into a silo for storage. The black PTO shaft extending from a tractor powers the unloading mechanism.

Lee Klancher

1928 McCORMICK-DEERING 15-30

Top Speed:
4.0 miles per hour

Weight:
6,000 pounds

Horsepower:
34.91 belt horsepower

Length:
11 feet 5 inches

FUN FACT

The McCormick-Deering 15-30 was so well designed it stayed useful for 10 years or more!

Height: 5 feet 10 inches

Width: 5 feet 5 inches

Lee Klancher

A boy fills up a tractor with gas. A full tank on an early Farmall was about 13 gallons. Compare that with some modern tractors that can hold about 500 gallons! *Library of Congress 2017719878*

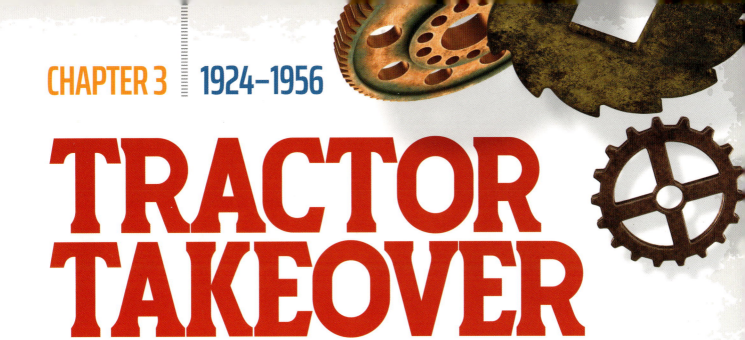

CHAPTER 3 | 1924–1956

TRACTOR TAKEOVER

In 1927, Frank Thompson sobs as he watches his father lead Jake, the horse, into the trailer. The nine-year-old spent so many mornings with Jake, feeding him before a long day of work. Frank doesn't understand. How can they turn out a member of their own family?

Frank's father is sad to see Jake go too. But they can't afford to feed him, especially now that they have their own tractor. The tractor can do everything the horse can, and it doesn't need to eat. Instead, it runs on cheap gas. The one thing a tractor

1944 Farmall Model H.
Lee Klancher

Tractors relied on cheap fuel such as kerosene to operate. Horses and mules required grain to survive, which took many acres to grow. *Wisconsin Historical Society 49196*

doesn't do is stop when you yell, "Whoa!" Frank's dad found that out when he accidentally mowed over a fence with the tractor.

In the late 1910s, International Harvester Company (IH) engineers saw their real competition came not only from the Fordson, but also from the horse. They wanted to replace all the horses on the farm. Alarmed, an anti-tractor organization emerged in 1919.

BY THE NUMBERS

SAVING TIME

To grow crops, farmers need to prepare the ground, plant, and harvest. The number of bushels of wheat they could produce with 10 hours of work more than tripled between 1920 and 1950. Technology was a big reason.

37.0 BUSHELS
22.7 BUSHELS
14.3 BUSHELS
11.1 BUSHELS

1920 — TOOLS: GAS TRACTOR, TRACTOR-PULLED BINDER, TRACTOR-POWERED THRESHER

1930 — TOOLS: 3-BOTTOM GANG PLOW, TRACTOR-PULLED CULTIVATOR, 12-FOOT COMBINE

1940 — TOOLS: 10-FOOT PLOW, TRACTOR-PULLED CULTIVATOR, ONE-MAN COMBINE

1950 — TOOLS: 10-FOOT PLOW, 12-FOOT CULTIVATOR, 14-FOOT DRILL, SELF-PROPELLED COMBINE

The bar graph above shows how many bushels could be harvested in a 10-hour period in each year. Can you figure out the number of bushels harvested in one hour for each given year?

Here's how you would do it:

$$\frac{11.1 \text{ BUSHELS}}{10 \text{ HOURS}} = 1.1 \text{ BUSHELS AN HOUR}$$

Source: Cooper, Barton, and Brodell. Progress of Farm Mechanization. USDA, 1947.

OUT TO PASTURE

As the tractor became more helpful, more farmers said goodbye to their horses and mules.

What trends do you see in this graph?

In what year are there nearly the same number of tractors and animals?

HORSES AND MULES ON FARMS — TRACTORS ON FARMS

Sources: USDA 1962 Agricultural Statistics and Census p. 432, Historical Statistics, p. 469 https://www.census.gov/library/publications/1960/compendia/hist_stats_colonial-1957.html

A GROWING COUNTRY

The population of the United States increased by almost 50 million between 1920 and 1950. But the number of farmers decreased. What reasons can you think of for this difference?

Year	US Population	US Farm Population
1920	111,271,341	10,790,000
1930	128,119,335	8,441,000
1940	138,601,511	7,589,000
1950	158,804,397	6,402,000

Source: https://ourworldindata.org/employment-in-agriculture#number-of-people-working-in-agriculture
Source: https://ourworldindata.org/grapher/population-past-future?tab=chart&country=POL~USA~PRT~PYF

The Horse Association of America encouraged the use of horses and mules and **lobbied** to keep heavy tractors off roads. It fought to protect jobs connected with horses, like saddle makers, carriage drivers, and stable owners.

In the end, the work was for nothing. Between 1920 and 1930, seven million horses left American farms. The trend began in 1923 with IH's release of the Farmall, an all-purpose tractor. The Great Depression of the 1930s slowed down tractor purchases. But then, World War II took men and women out of the fields and into the war effort. With fewer people, farmers needed tractor power. And as the number of tractors grew, the number of horses dropped.

By the mid-1900s, tractors outnumbered horses on the farm. Tractor sales peaked in 1951. IH built its one-millionth Farmall that same year. Tractor power had arrived.

Children watch a tractor baling hay in 1944. By the 1940s the tractor had mostly replaced the farm horse.
Library of Congress 2017866429

FARMING THROUGH THE AGES

Library of Congress LC-H813-F02-030

1919 — The Horse Association of America is formed to promote the use of horses and mules over tractors.

1923 — IH releases the Farmall, the first general-purpose tractor.

1928 — Harry Ferguson invents the three-point hitch.

National Archives 306-NT-165.319C

1929 — A stock market crash marks the beginning of the Great Depression.

Library of Congress LC-DIG-fsa-8b38290

1930 — The Dust Bowl begins and lasts until 1939 when rains return.

1939 — The Farmall Letter Series debuts.

Library of Congress LC-USZ62-16555

1941 — The US joins World War II after the attack on Pearl Harbor on December 7. The war ends in 1945.

1942 — IH launches the H-10-H cotton harvester, the first successful mechanical cotton picker.

Lee Klancher

1942 — IH builds the first self-propelled combine, the No. 123-SP.

1947 — IH introduces the smaller Farmall Cub tractor line.

Lee Klancher

1951 — Tractor sales peak in the US and IH builds its one millionth Farmall tractor.

1928 THE FRIENDLY FARMALL

Frank Thompson, only 10 years old, is nervous. Today, he will drive the tractor through the fields to cultivate. Cultivation means breaking up dirt around plants. This helps plants grow by destroying weeds and allowing more water and air into the softer soil.

His dad tells him that he's ready. But cultivating is tricky. The front wheels of the tractor only just fit in between the rows of crops. Frank must drive the tractor perfectly through the field, or risk pulling up the cotton his family just planted.

Before 1923, tractors could pull a plow and turn a belt, but they couldn't cultivate. The tractors weren't tall enough to drive over tall crops. That meant that farmers still needed a horse. Finally, an answer to that problem came with the arrival of the Farmall. The Farmall was the first general-purpose tractor, and it had taller rear wheels so it could plow, harvest, cultivate, and so much more. For the next 30 years, every tractor looked a lot like the Farmall.

A young boy drives a Farmall tractor with a cultivator attached to the back. *Wisconsin Historical Society 47366*

A farmer plows a field with a Farmall in Idaho. The Farmall was the first tractor that could replace a horse on the farm because it was able to cultivate, plow, and power equipment. *Dorothea Lang / Library of Congress LC-DIG-FSA-8B35395*

Engineer Bert R. Benjamin was the main force behind the Farmall. In the 1910s, Benjamin began dreaming of a machine that could finally replace a horse. But his test tractors looked odd and didn't work smoothly. Many people at IH wanted Benjamin to stop working on his project. They had spent a lot of money building McCormick-Deerings and didn't want the Farmall to steal any sales away.

Benjamin never gave up and by 1920 his engineering team had a test model that ran eleven farming **implements**, or tools, attached to the tractor. The International 8-16 could only run four implements without help from horses or more people. Despite this, the bosses at IH

POWER MOVES: COMPONENTS OF A TRACTOR

Tractors generate power and use it to pull and power farming implements. The power is generated by an engine and travels through the clutch, transmission, and final drive to the wheels. Most early tractors powered only the two rear wheels, while more modern machines often had all four wheels powered for more traction.

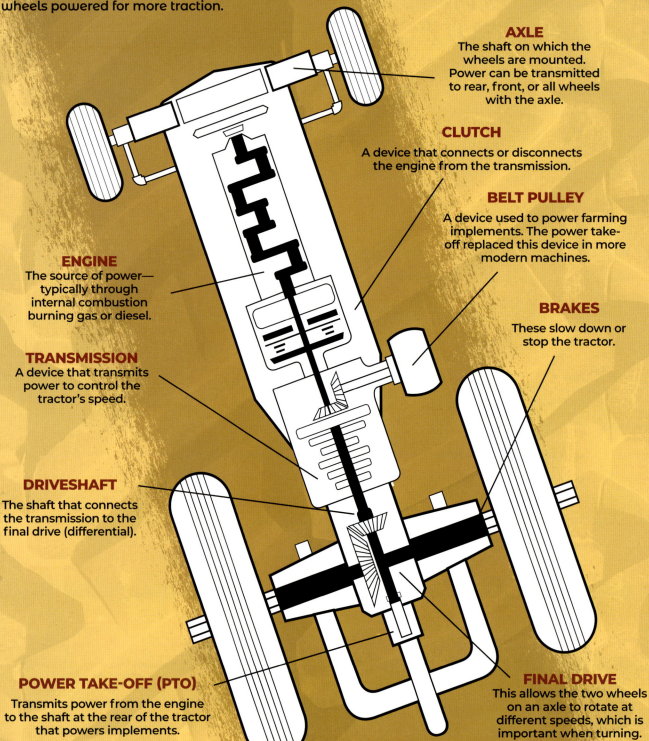

AXLE
The shaft on which the wheels are mounted. Power can be transmitted to rear, front, or all wheels with the axle.

CLUTCH
A device that connects or disconnects the engine from the transmission.

BELT PULLEY
A device used to power farming implements. The power take-off replaced this device in more modern machines.

ENGINE
The source of power—typically through internal combustion burning gas or diesel.

BRAKES
These slow down or stop the tractor.

TRANSMISSION
A device that transmits power to control the tractor's speed.

DRIVESHAFT
The shaft that connects the transmission to the final drive (differential).

POWER TAKE-OFF (PTO)
Transmits power from the engine to the shaft at the rear of the tractor that powers implements.

FINAL DRIVE
This allows the two wheels on an axle to rotate at different speeds, which is important when turning.

were unimpressed. The economy wasn't great and tractor sales were suffering. But the head of IH engineering had a hunch that Benjamin was on to something big and allowed him to keep working on the project.

In 1923, the Farmall was finally ready to be sold to farmers. Many of the first Farmalls were sent to Texas. Texas farmers loved their Farmalls. They wrote a letter to the president of IH threatening to build their own Farmalls if IH didn't produce more.

The most revolutionary feature was that a Farmall could cultivate, thanks to its design. Its narrow front wheels and tall frame allowed it to pass over crops without destroying them. Early Farmalls were gray with red wheels. The iconic "red tractor" wouldn't emerge until 1936.

In 1926, Farmall sales began to take off. By 1930, IH was building 200 a day. Other tractor makers scrambled to build a competitor. Because of his determination, Bert Benjamin had succeeded. He built an all-purpose tractor that became the blueprint for all future tractors.

Frank's family bought a Farmall in 1927 for their Texas farm. Now, his biggest test lies ahead of him. The 10-year-old looks at the field, taking a deep breath. This is his chance to prove himself. Frank shifts into gear and rolls toward the crops. Slowly and steadily, he drives straight down the row.

Case IH

THE ALL-PURPOSE TRACTOR: FARMING IMPLEMENTS

On a 200-acre farm, a farmer with a Farmall tractor could replace up to 18 horses and two or three men. The different implements helped! Even now, farmers buy a wide variety of attachments for their tractors. Here are some popular ones.

A Farmall could:
Plow 7-9 acres each day
Mow 50-60 acres in one day
Double disk 18-25 acres per day
Drill 45 acres per day
Plant 50 acres per day
Cultivate 30-50 acres per day

Plow:
A tool that cuts and breaks the soil to prepare it for planting. Plows are especially useful in land that has never been farmed before.

Wisconsin Historical Society 79780

Mower:
A machine that cuts down grasses and plants.

Wisconsin Historical Society 44580

Disc harrow:
A cutting machine that breaks up large clods of soil and prepares it for planting.

Wisconsin Historical Society 121751

Seed drill:
A tool that plants smaller grains, such as wheat, in closely spaced rows.

Wisconsin Historical Society 139370

Planter:
A device that plants larger seeds, such as peas, in rows.

Wisconsin Historical Society 133228

Cultivator:
A machine that mixes soil to allow for more water and air to seep in and breaks up weeds around crops.

Wisconsin Historical Society 129561

FUN FACT

Early Farmalls were painted gray with red wheels. But beginning in 1936, Farmalls were painted all red. The bright color made them visible on public roads, which kept farmers safe. Bright colored tractors also sold better.

Top Speed:
4.0 miles per hour

Weight:
4,000 pounds

Horsepower:
20.05 belt horsepower

Length:
11 feet 4 inches

Lee Klancher

1928 FARMALL REGULAR

Height: 5 feet 7 inches

Width: 7 feet 4 inches

1935 | THE GREAT DEPRESSION

Frank looks at the dusty sky. It's been a bad year. Heck, it's been a bad five years. Since 1930, a terrible drought has settled over the land and there hasn't been enough rain for crops to grow. Now, Frank's family can't grow cotton. It's too dry and dusty.

The 1930s were not good for farming. This time was called the Great Depression. Prices kept dropping. Farmers couldn't get a fair price to even cover the cost of harvesting their crops. So, food was left to rot. In Oregon, thousands of bushels of apples sat untouched in the orchards. In Montana, thousands of bushels of wheat were left unharvested in fields.

Farmers could barely hold onto their farms, much less buy a brand-new tractor. As a response to the Great Depression, tractor companies built fewer tractors during the 1930s. Total tractor sales in the US dropped from 200,000 in 1930 to 19,000 in 1932. Despite the low sales, IH had enough cash to improve its tractors. They had sold plenty of tractors and farming equipment in the past 30 years. The company also managed its money wisely. IH spent the 1930s developing new technology and improving their designs.

In 1932, IH was the number one tractor maker. John Deere was second, and J. I. Case was third. After the Farmall appeared, competitors hurried to make a general-purpose tractor. Competition was starting to get fierce. IH was still number one, but John Deere and J. I. Case were gaining ground. IH wanted a boost to stay on top.

A farmer drives a Farmall H tractor and pulls a combine behind him to harvest wheat. *Wisconsin Historical Society 2487*

Children pile onto a truck in Kansas in 1939. Once the rains returned, the Dust Bowl ended and the future looked brighter. *Library of Congress LC-DIG-FSA-8A26911*

The Farmall Letter Series was the answer. IH hired Raymond Loewy, a famous designer, to redesign the Farmall's look. Before working on the tractor, he had designed logos, refrigerators, and train engines. The result was a modernized look. The new Farmalls had a rounded hood and slotted grille. A streamlined sheet of metal covered the radiator, fuel tank, and top of the engine.

Loewy also thought about the driver when he was designing the new Farmalls. He moved the engine to the left so the driver could see the ground while cultivating. The seat was more comfortable too. No more busted jeans! The new design gave IH an edge over the competition and the Farmall continued to be the top-selling—and most iconic—tractor for years to come.

Frank's family fights bitterly to keep the land. They're lucky to have stores of grain and enough cash to keep them afloat. But many families move away to find work. Before a neighbor moves, he offers to sell his tractor. But it's buried under so much dirt the buyer must dig it out. Frank's family holds on, and the rains finally come again in 1939. Maybe now they can afford one of those brand-new Farmalls!

THE DUST BOWL

Farm auctions were common in the 1930s. At this auction, police were called to prevent neighbors from chasing off real bidders and preventing the sale. *Library of Congress LC-DIG-fsa-8b08252*

Average Income Per Farm

Farmers' Income Steadily Declines

During the early 1930s, farmers' incomes dropped dramatically. Many couldn't repay their loans to the bank. To make up for the money lost, banks took the farmers' possessions and sold them to the highest bidder at events called foreclosure auctions.

Farmers were fed up. They banded together and showed up at their neighbors' foreclosure auctions. To help the family that had lost everything to the bank, they kept bids for possessions very low. That way the farmers might be able to buy back their things.

When someone wanted to offer more for a plow or tractor, farmers would physically hold the bidder back from bidding. These auctions where banks hardly made any money were called "penny auctions."

Consequences of Technology: To Plow or Not to Plow?

Across the Great Plains in the 1930s, strong winds picked up millions of tons of soil and blew it across the prairie. The area became known as the Dust Bowl. On some days, the whole sky turned black. To feed the chickens, families tied a rope between the house and the coop, so they wouldn't get lost. They hung sheets over the windows and tied rags around their faces to keep the dust out, but to no avail. The dirt collected everywhere—on plates, cups, and in people's noses. Many families moved away because they couldn't survive.

Where did the dust come from? It turns out, it was an unintentional side effect of drought, the post-war economy, technology, and the plow. To make up for low crop prices after World War I, farmers broke more ground and grew even more crops. Tractors and other farming inventions helped farmers quickly tear up prairie grass and plant more cash crops.

At the time, most farmers plowed right after a harvest. With enough rain, this wasn't a problem. But when the soil dried out, winds could blow entire fields of dirt away. About 850 million tons of soil blew off the Plains in 1935 alone.

Today, some farmers use a no-till system to prevent soil from blowing or washing away. Plowing can also kill beneficial creatures like earthworms. And not plowing means less work and fuel! But plowing has its benefits. It breaks up the soil and gives roots room to grow. It can help with water drainage and add nutrients to the soil. Farmers must decide what works best for them.

In western Oklahoma, a boy tries to not breathe in dust. Dust entered houses and caused serious illnesses in many people during this time. *Library of Congress LC-USF34-004047-E*

The dust was so severe it was difficult to see and walk. It piled up against houses and even buried farm machines. *Library of Congress LC-USZC4-4840*

FUN FACT

The small Farmall A and B were the first models in the Farmall line to receive a sleek new look created by famous industrial designer Raymond Loewy. The bright pink color on this Farmall A is not original to the tractor. The color was changed later by collectors to support breast cancer awareness!

Width: 6 feet 5 inches

Lee Klancher

1944 FARMALL A

Height: 5 feet 3 inches

Top Speed: 10.0 miles per hour

Horsepower: 18.34 belt horsepower

Weight: 2,400 pounds

Length: 8 feet 10 inches

1941 | WORLD WAR II

By 1941, life is looking rosier. Rains have returned and the crops are growing. Frank is married to Elizabeth and now they have a farm and a two-year-old son named Douglas.

However, better times must wait. Frank and Elizabeth sit near the radio waiting for the news. Japan has bombed Pearl Harbor in Hawaii as a direct attack on the nation. After the bombing, America enters World War II. Frank and Elizabeth are shocked.

Frank is called to serve in the army and Elizabeth must work the farm without him. Nearly two million men and women from farming families served in the armed forces. That left a shortage of workers at home. But people still needed food. US farmers had to feed the country, its soldiers, and millions of people around the world.

This ad was created to promote Victory Gardens during World War II. People in the US were encouraged to help the war effort by growing their own food. *Wisconsin Historical Society 4762*

To address the shortage, the Women's Land Army reassembled. About three million non-farm women deployed to the fields to grow crops. In 1942, IH started a program to teach women about tractors. These "Tractorettes" learned how to operate farm equipment like tractors and harvesters.

Elizabeth joins the Tractorette program. Growing up on a farm, she knows a lot. Impressed, the teacher tests her one day by putting water in the gas line of the tractor. Elizabeth figures out the problem in minutes!

At a time when tractors were needed the most to make up for fewer farmers, the US government asked tractor companies to slow down their production. Raw materials like steel were in short supply because they were needed for the war effort. Factories were converted to build tanks, airplanes, and other military supplies.

Eventually, the government recognized that combines could help harvest more food with fewer people. So, they allowed more to be made. Before the war, many farmers considered

Three women work on a tractor during Tractorette training. *Wisconsin Historical Society 27316*

combines to be a luxury. They were very expensive! But the war and the loss of farmworkers made them necessary.

In 1942, IH introduced its first self-propelled combine, the No. 123-SP. With this machine a farmer could harvest 100 bushels of wheat with only 34 hours of labor, compared to 300 hours in 1830. The combine automatically reaped, threshed, and winnowed grain. It was more **fuel-efficient**, which means it took less fuel compared to pull-behind combines.

Even though it feels like a luxury, Elizabeth buys a combine. It's a huge help to harvest the wheat crop. She is careful to keep the combine clean, or else leaves and chaff can build up around the engine and light on fire! Elizabeth can't afford for that to happen. Combine fires are common and farmers must maintain their machines to prevent this.

The war changed so much for so many people. Families lost sons, brothers, fathers, and husbands. The day Frank comes home, Elizabeth whoops and runs toward him, jumping into his arms. The family is back together again!

A farmer harvests wheat with a self-propelled combine. The machine in this picture may be a prototype.
Wisconsin Historical Society 7777

THE BRACEROS

To help fill the labor gap, the US government made an agreement with Mexico to allow Mexican laborers to work on US farms. Starting in 1942, millions of Mexican men traveled north to work the farms. The program was called the Bracero Program, which comes from the Spanish word *brazo* for arm. From 1942 until the program's end in 1964, more than 4 million braceros worked in the US.

Mexico and the US agreed on rules meant to protect braceros from poor wages and poor treatment. Workers were supposed to receive a guaranteed wage and were not supposed to pay for their living expenses. Unfortunately, many were treated poorly and experienced discrimination. Many were charged extra for room and board, earned lower wages than they were promised, and were exposed to deadly chemicals.

Braceros pick beets near Stockton, California. Mexico and the US were allies in World War II. The program began after the US asked Mexico to help with farm labor during the war.
Library of Congress LC-DIG-fsa-8d29109

HOW TRANSMISSIONS WORK

Transmissions are part of the system that transfers power from the engine to the wheels in a vehicle. The transmission's role is to vary the speed at which power is delivered, which in turn changes the speed of the vehicle.

Transmissions have different gears, or speeds. Early tractors have as few as three or four speeds, while later tractors have 20 or more different speeds.

When a tractor is in a high gear, it moves more quickly but cannot pull with as much force. Higher gears are good for traveling quickly, for example, when driving a tractor from the field to the farm on a road.

When a tractor is in a low gear, it has more power but can't move as fast. Lower gears are good for pulling plows or other situations that require a lot of machine muscle.

Most older tractors used manual transmissions, meaning the operator selected the appropriate gear for the job.

More modern tractors have transmissions that automatically adjust the speed.

Most early tractors used mechanical gear-drive transmissions. They changed speeds by transferring power through different-sized gears. Gear-drive transmissions are quite complex, with a dozen or more different gears that can be moved to provide different speeds.

Most gear-drive transmissions require the driver to press the clutch pedal to disengage the engine, move the shift lever to the preferred gear, then release the clutch pedal. Newer tractors are designed so that a driver can shift without depressing a clutch, and most large farm tractors shift automatically using sophisticated electronically controlled transmissions.

GEAR SHIFT
Used to change gear selection.

OUTPUT SHAFT
Power goes out to the final drive.

INPUT SHAFT
Connected to the engine, which drives the transmission.

1952 McCORMICK-DEERING NO. 127-SP

FUN FACT
The 127-SP was very similar to the No. 123-SP, which was IHC's first self-propelled combine.

Top Speed:
13.3 miles per hour

Horsepower:
49 horsepower

Width:
13 feet 6 inches

Wisconsin Historical Society 24613

1950 | TRACTORS COME HOME

Eleven-year-old Douglas and his younger brothers run home as fast as they can after school. Today's the big day. They're getting a new tractor! When they get home, they see a gleaming red machine in the drive. The kids yell with delight and climb all over it, fighting to see who can sit in the seat first.

The period after World War II was a high point for tractor companies. More tractors were sold at that point in history than any other time. Many men came home from the war familiar with machines like tanks or airplanes. Running a tractor seemed like second nature.

The Farmall Super C was part of the Farmall Letter Series. Almost 100,000 were built between 1951 and 1954.
Wisconsin Historical Society 8868

A farmer shells corn with a machine that's powered by a Farmall C tractor. This one is using a belt, but a power take-off (PTO) shaft could also be used to power the corn sheller. *Wisconsin Historical Society 8677*

Farmers also needed the extra help from tractors. After World War II, the economy was booming, and farmers still had to feed the country... and the world. Plus, 1.5 million families moved off their farms for city jobs. Many who remained bought their neighbors' land and needed bigger equipment to work more land. Soon, 300 acres was considered a small farm. Grain, corn, and soybean farms often were as large as 1,000 acres!

For a farmer of more than 100 acres, the Model H and Model M were the best choices. They performed many jobs, like pulling a feed wagon, plowing, cultivating, and more. These models were so popular that IH sold almost one million of them in all.

In the 1940s, there were still farmers who were working the land with draft animals or by hand. There was a lag in tractor sales, especially in the Deep South where there were more small farms. Seeing that there was still a need for a smaller, more **maneuverable** tractor, IH introduced the Farmall Cub in 1947. The small tractor was aimed toward "single mule" farmers, and it was a success. Between 1947 and 1964, IH built 200,000 of the original Cub. The line continued until 1981. Now any farmer could own a tractor.

By the 1950s, the tractor industry had settled on several design standards. One of the features that took the tractor world by storm was the **three-point hitch**. In the 1920s, it was a big task to hook up a tool to a tractor. Making a turn was not simple. When a farmer got to

PICKING COTTON

One region to experience major changes after the war was the South. Farming the South's most popular crop, cotton, was mostly done by hand. But between 1910 and 1970, many people, especially Black Americans, moved out of the South. People left farms to look for jobs in cities, especially in the North. Southern farms scrambled for machines to fill in the labor gaps.

Enter the mechanical cotton picker. IH launched the first successful mechanical cotton picker, the H-10-H, in 1942. Handpicking an acre of cotton took 125 hours, but the machines dropped that number to 25. Most of the nation's cotton was still handpicked in the 1950s. By the late 1960s, almost all was harvested by machines.

A farmer drives a McCormick-Deering H-10-H cotton picker. John Rust, the inventor of the cotton picker, had picked cotton as a boy and wanted to save others from the back-breaking work. *Wisconsin Historical Society 78138*

TRACTOR TURNOVERS

Tractor flips are related to a tractor's **center of gravity**. An object's center of gravity is where its weight is the same on each side. Tractors flip backward when the front of the tractor lifts off the ground until the tractor's center of gravity passes the "point of no return." After that, a back flip is unavoidable. Tractors can reach the point of no return in less than a second.

Center of Gravity: The weight of an object is concentrated at its center. That is also the point where the object can be balanced. What does that mean? It means you can find the center of gravity of any object by balancing it. Let's try!

What you'll need:

- A table
- A ruler
- A hammer
- String (something thicker than thread) or a rubber band

Instructions:

Create a loop with the string (or use the rubber band) and set up the ruler, hammer, and loop like in the diagram below.

Rest the ruler on the table and hold it lightly in place with one hand while you move the loop along the hammer to discover where it balances.

Make sure the handle of the hammer is touching the ruler.

Once you find that "magic" spot where the ruler and hammer balance like in the diagram and you can remove your hand, you have successfully found the hammer's center of gravity! That means that the same amount of mass (for the hammer) is on either side of the loop.

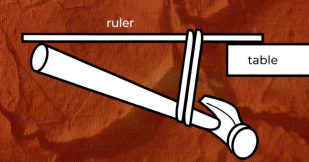

Raymond Loewy sketched the new IH logo while on a train from Chicago to New York. It was meant to look like a person driving a tractor. Can you see it? You can still see a slanted version of the logo on every Case IH machine. *Wisconsin Historical Society 37635*

the end of a row, he'd get off the tractor, raise the tool, make the turn, get down, and drop the tool onto the ground. With the three-point hitch, tools were now mounted on the tractor, instead of pulled behind. A system of **hydraulics** helped lift and lower the tool without the farmer even getting off the tractor.

Douglas's father has brought the Model M home. Douglas can't believe this shiny new tractor is theirs! He can't wait until his father lets him drive it.

1954 FARMALL SUPER M-TA

Top Speed: 16.75 miles per hour

Weight: 5,500 pounds

Horsepower: 46 belt horsepower

Width: 7 feet

FUN FACT

The Farmall Super M-TA was a popular tractor, but its predecessor, the Farmall M, sold more than 270,000 units, making it one of the best-selling full-size red tractors ever built.

Height: 6 feet 7 inches

Length: 12 feet 1 inch

Lee Klancher

In the 1970s, Steiger tractors provided farmers with the power they needed. Steiger released this red, white, and blue tractor in 1976 to celebrate the United States's 200th birthday. *Scott Anderson Collection*

CHAPTER 4 | 1957–1978

HORSEPOWER WARS

In the spring of 1957, 11-year-old Linda watches as her best friend, Gary, piles into the car with his family. Gary lived on the farm next door. He and Linda had spent many afternoons chasing each other, climbing stacks of hay bales, and playing hide and seek.

His parents have decided to sell the farm and move to the city. Linda's family bought their farm. She sighs. She'll be lonely without her friend. And she'll have to work more to farm the extra land. Linda's parents will need to buy a more powerful tractor to handle more acres.

At the time of its introduction, the International 4300 was the most powerful tractor on the market. But it wasn't popular. Fewer than 50 were built. *Lee Klancher*

BY THE NUMBERS

Farming Goes Big

As the 1900s progressed, farming became even more efficient, and the average farm grew larger. One farmer could feed many more people in 1970 than 150 years earlier.

Average Number of People One Farmer Can Feed

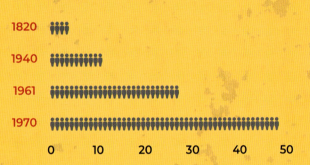

A Growing Country

The number of farmers decreased by over half from the mid- to late-1900s. Meanwhile, the US population boomed. What did that mean for farming?

Year	US Population	US Farm Population
1940	138,601,511	7,589,000
1950	158,804,397	6,402,000
1960	186,720,570	4,531,000
1970	209,513,340	3,118,000
1980	229,476,360	3,275,000

Source: https://ourworldindata.org/employment-in-agriculture#number-of-people-working-in-agriculture

Source: https://ourworldindata.org/grapher/population-past-future?tab=chart&country=POL~USA~PRT~PYF

BIGGER AND STRONGER

Early tractors were massive and heavy compared to their horsepower. Notice that although the tractors in 1906 and 1958 are almost the same weight, the horsepower is very different.

Year	Tractor	Weight	Engine Horsepower
1906	Friction-Drive Tractor	13,500 pounds	20
1915	Case 65 Steam Tractor	20,600 pounds	65
1924	Farmall Regular	4,000 pounds	20
1939	Farmall M	4,858 pounds	33
1958	Steiger #1	15,000 pounds	238

SOURCE: https://www.sdstate.edu/south-dakota-agricultural-heritage-museum/1915-j-i-case-steam-engine-65-hp

Farming changed dramatically during the 1960s and 1970s. Scientists developed new technologies, such as hardy crop varieties and **herbicides** to prevent weeds from growing. Farmers were harvesting more than ever. Then, in 1970, droughts around the world led to a steep rise in demand for US crops. Prices soared and farmers prospered.

Many were eager to use their earnings to buy new tractors. Increasing horsepower became important to farmers. Farmers needed more power to replace the people who had moved away. In 1960, the average farm tractor had 40–50 horsepower. Today, that is the average for **compact**, or smaller, tractors.

International Harvester Company (IH) realized that farmers wanted more powerful tractors than the company had been offering. IH introduced two models with higher horsepower.

The International 660 produced 81-horsepower, making it IH's biggest row-crop tractor in the late 1950s. But only about 7,000 were built. Why? The market demanded more power! Farmers wanted machines with 100 horsepower or more. *Lee Klancher*

But there was a problem with some of these tractors. IH hadn't tested them enough. Soon, farmers were returning to the dealers with broken parts. IH engineers worked overtime to fix the problem, but IH's reputation had taken a hit.

That doesn't mean that IH didn't sell tractors. Farmers were loyal to their red tractors! But in the 1960s and 1970s IH had fierce competition. Many tractor companies tried to outdo each other in the horsepower wars. Over the next twenty years, tractors became even bigger and more powerful.

A woman drives an International 454 as it pulls a hay baler. *Wisconsin Historical Society 8722*

FARMING THROUGH THE AGES

Ken Ohnell Collection

1958 — The Steiger family builds their first tractor, which has a higher horsepower than most of the machines on the market at that time.

1958 — The Farmall 460 and 560 are introduced but need to be recalled.

1960 — IH buys Solar Aircraft, a company that builds turbine engines and other parts for spacecraft.

1961 — The Soviet Union launches the first man into space, Yuri Gagarin.

1961 — IH debuts the HT-340, a hydrostatic, turbine engine tractor.

Case IH

1962 — Cesar Chavez fights for migrant farmworker's rights in California.

1963 — President John F. Kennedy is assassinated on November 22nd.

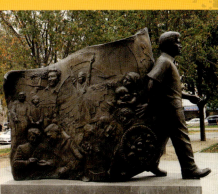
Library of Congress LC-DIG-highsm-23135

1965 — The International 1206 is the first IH two-wheel-drive tractor to break the 100-horsepower barrier.

1969 — US astronauts Neil Armstrong, "Buzz" Aldrin, and Michael Collins land on the moon. IH's division, Solar Industries, provides parts for the mission.

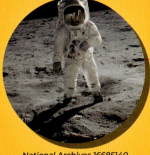
National Archives 16685140

1973 — IH begins to sell Steiger-built four-wheel-drive tractors.
Case IH

1973 — An energy crisis causes long lines and low supplies of diesel fuel.

1977 — The launch of the Axial Flow Combine transforms the combine industry.

Lee Klancher

95

1957 GAINING TRACTION

Linda collapses into bed. She and her family have been working nonstop for the past two days. Heavy rains are threatening to flood the farm. To protect their property, she and her family haul sandbags to the creek's edge to keep it from flooding. But when the creek begins to flow over the sandbags, they change their strategy.

The family parks their **two-wheel-drive** tractors and trucks on a hilltop so they won't wash away in the flood. The family also empties one grain bin and moves the grain to the barn loft. But there is too much grain and not enough time to empty the second. They are going to lose a lot of the summer's harvest.

Linda and her family weren't the only Minnesotans to face flooding in 1957. People fled Minneapolis and St. Paul because of the rising water. After the floods, fields were a muddy mess. Farmers didn't dare drive their tractors into fields because they'd get stuck in the mud. But farmers with **four-wheel drive** could risk it.

The Steiger family built their first tractor after looking at a 100+ horsepower Wagner tractor. They figured that they could build a tractor for less than the Wagner's $20,000 price tag. *Lee Klancher*

Four-wheel drive means all four wheels are powered by the engine. This gives vehicles better **traction**, or grip, over uneven land. Big farms were having a hard time finding equipment with enough power and traction to work the fields. Some farmers swapped out engines. Others combined two tractors or construction equipment to make their own powerful four-wheel drives.

Four-wheel-drive tractors were slow to come to the tractor market. In the 1910s, IH engineers added four-wheel drive to some International 8-16s. But they had a flawed design that caused the machines to lose traction rather than gain it. IH stopped offering the feature for the International 8-16s.

Douglass and Maurice Steiger and their father, John, wanted a large four-wheel-drive tractor for their 5,200-acre farm. Frustrated with the cost of available tractors on the market, they built their own. They had already made machines like a 60-foot weed sprayer. Why not a tractor?

IH tried out machines that powered more than four wheels to give it more traction. Here's an experimental tractor from 1937 that provided power to 6 sets of wheels! *Wisconsin Historical Society 12199*

HOW DO FOUR-WHEEL-DRIVE TRACTORS WORK?

Four-wheel drive means that power is sent to both the front and rear wheels of a vehicle. How does it work?

The power travels along this route: from the engine to the transmission, then to the drive shafts, and finally to the front and rear wheels. Not all the engine power goes to the wheels all the time, however.

On both the front and rear axles, the power needs to be distributed between the right and left wheels to easily turn the vehicle.

When a car makes a left turn, the wheels on the right need to travel a farther distance than the wheels on the left. So the right wheels spin faster than the left. The **differential** sends different amounts of power to each wheel, so they can spin at different speeds.

For the most traction, however, all the power needs to go to all the wheels at the same time. To do this, the differential needs to be locked, with all the wheels spinning at the same speed. This provides tremendous traction. It's used in tough situations, like pulling a heavy load up a muddy hill.

Tractor differential locks are either applied manually or automatically as conditions require.

The parts of a four-wheel-drive system are:

REAR DRIVESHAFT
A rod that connects the engine to the rear differential.

FRONT DRIVESHAFT
A rod that connects the engine to the front differential.

REAR DIFFERENTIAL
Sends power from the transmission to the back wheels.

TRANSFER CASE
Divides the power between the front and rear axles.

FRONT DIFFERENTIAL
Sends power from the transmission to the front wheels.

There are different ways to deliver power to all four wheels. Here are the two types of true four-wheel-drive tractors:

ARTICULATED: These tractors bend in the middle. **Articulated** tractors are easier to maintain and more durable than rigid frame tractors. Today, all true four-wheel-drive tractors are articulated.

RIGID FRAME: These tractors came equipped with different driving modes: front steer, rear steer, and coordinated, where axles worked together to drive the tractor in a tight circle. These were phased out in favor of articulated tractors.

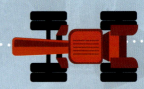

The team began working in their small dairy barn in western Minnesota in the fall of 1957. Fifty-seven days later, they had a four-wheel-drive tractor with an engine that produced 238 horsepower. It was one of the first farm tractors to pass 200 horsepower.

The barn was barely big enough to fit the tractor. The large tractor they built proved to be exactly what they needed! That spring, the Steiger brothers cultivated 300 acres in one 15-hour day. The machine did the work of all three of the family's smaller IH tractors. It was so strong that it could pull 12 plows at a time!

Local farmers wanted in. They started asking for smaller, 100-horsepower Steiger tractors. The brothers began building their powerful, four-wheel-drive tractors out of a plant in Fargo, North Dakota.

POWERING THE WHEELS

For any moving vehicle, engines must deliver power to the wheels. Chapter 3 talks about how power is transferred from the transmission to the wheels. The final drive is the last step. In two-wheel-drive vehicles, the final drive delivers power to two wheels. In four-wheel drives, the final drive powers all four wheels.

How Does a Final Drive Work?

Torque from the engine turns the drive shaft, which then connects to the final drive. The final drive then turns the drive **axles**, which rotate the wheels and move the tractor.

Torque is the amount of force needed to turn an object around its center, but what does that mean? Try this experiment as a demonstration of "applying torque":

Find a container in your house with a screw top, like a peanut butter or pickle jar. Can you unscrew the jar? If you can, you were applying torque, or the force required to turn the lid. Now, have someone stronger than you close the jar as tight as they can. Try to open it again. Is it harder? Can you feel your muscles working harder? You are applying more torque, or more power, to unscrew the jar.

The same thing is happening in an engine. The difference is, with the jar, you are turning the lid around its own center to unscrew and open the jar. In an engine, torque is used to turn the driveshaft, which then turns the axles that then turns the wheels.

IH originally built final drives with chains that worked like the chains on a bicycle. The chains needed to be adjusted often. If they were too tight, the chain and sprockets would wear out quickly. If they were too loose, the chain would fall off. The company eventually switched the final drives to a gear-based system.

FINAL DRIVE

See page 66 for more detail.

1968 STEIGER 2200

FUN FACT

The Steiger 2200 was one of the first Steiger models sold to farmers. It was also one of the most popular of the barn-built machines.

Horsepower: 238 belt horsepower

Weight: 23,000 pounds

Top Speed: 16.0 miles per hour

Lee Klancher

Wheel base (axle to axle): 11 feet

1965 | TRACTORS DURING THE SPACE AGE

The 1960s were a decade of seismic change: In the South, protesters marched for equal rights for Black Americans, President John F. Kennedy was assassinated, and a rivalry with the Soviet Union spurred on the Space Race. After NASA was established in 1958, the entire country rallied behind the US government to beat the Soviet Union to the moon. Both countries made huge leaps in science and engineering. In 1961, the Soviet Union launched the first man into space, but the US pushed harder and in 1969 won the Space Race by landing the first men on the moon.

IH made amazing advancements during this era and even contributed to the moon mission. In 1960, the company bought a business called Solar Aircraft, which turned into IH's Solar Division. It went on to build many parts of the spacecraft that flew to the moon.

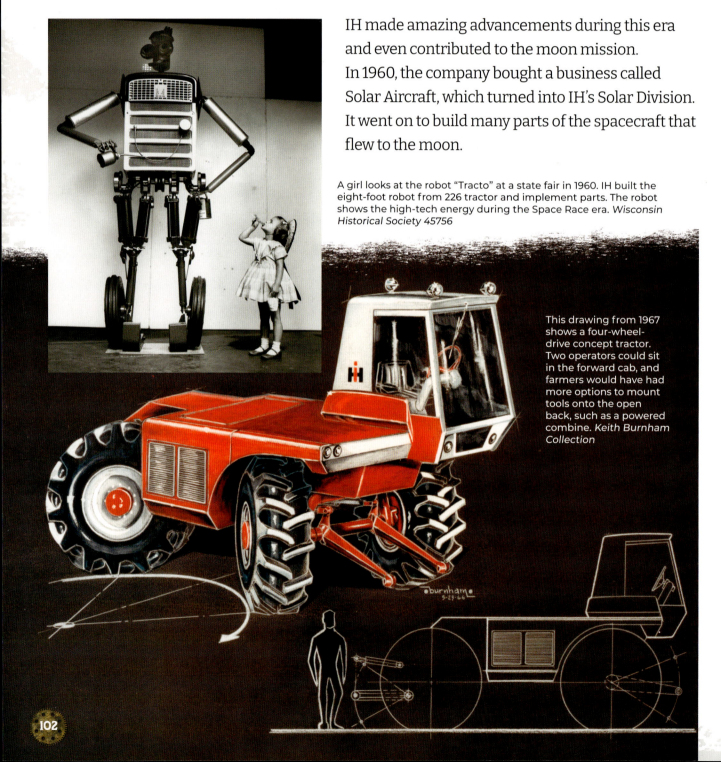

A girl looks at the robot "Tracto" at a state fair in 1960. IH built the eight-foot robot from 226 tractor and implement parts. The robot shows the high-tech energy during the Space Race era. *Wisconsin Historical Society 45756*

This drawing from 1967 shows a four-wheel-drive concept tractor. Two operators could sit in the forward cab, and farmers would have had more options to mount tools onto the open back, such as a powered combine. *Keith Burnham Collection*

Engineers from IH test the HT-340 tractor. The experimental machine was damaged in a car accident on the way home from its first public display in 1961. *Wisconsin Historical Society 75472*

Many of the technologies we use today came from NASA's inventions during the Space Race. Handheld vacuums, water filtration, and wireless headsets were all invented for the astronauts.

Linda remembers the day she heard about the first man in space. She was 15. It devastated her that the Soviet Union beat the US. That was the day she decided to become an engineer.

IH was changing too. The addition of the Solar Division helped the company focus on research and technology. Solar Aircraft built **turbine engines**. If you've flown on an airplane you've seen a gas turbine engine. Turbine engines use spinning fan blades that suck air into the engine. As the mix of air and gas burns, the exhaust gases spin the turbine and shoot out the back. The jet of air moves the machine forward.

IH tasked Solar Aircraft with a challenge: add a gas turbine engine into one of their new, high-tech **hydrostatic** tractors. Hydrostatic technology transfers power from the engine to the wheels by fluid instead of a geared transmission. To change speeds with a regular tractor, drivers used a clutch to shift gears. That often meant that the driver had to slow down or stop.

HYDRAULIC POWER

From tractors to airplanes, many machines depend on hydraulic power to work. The science of hydraulics depends on several features of liquids. Liquids can't be squeezed into a smaller space. But they can flow to fill any shape. Also, they will press on anything equally in all directions. Engineers have used these characteristics to perform hard tasks with less force.

For example, when someone squeezes a water gun trigger, they don't have to squeeze very hard or fast. But the liquid gets squeezed into a small tube and shoots out very fast because of hydraulic power.

SCIENCE OF HYDROSTATIC TRANSMISSION

Hydrostatic transmissions depend on the movement of oil instead of gears to power wheels. Chapter 3 explains how gears in a manual transmission work. A hydrostatic transmission does the same thing—it lets a vehicle change speed and power. But a hydrostatic transmission uses fluid instead of gears to transfer power. It also uses a complex system of shafts and chambers to change speed. Hydrostatic transmissions aren't stuck on specific speeds like many manual transmissions. Instead, drivers can move smoothly through different speeds. This gives drivers better control.

International Harvester equipped this turbine-engined HT-340 tractor with an experimental hydrostatic transmission. The turbine engine was not practical, but the hydrostatic transmission was excellent and used on several production tractors.
Wisconsin Historical Society / George Bowman / 11323

But with a hydrostatic drive, drivers easily shifted speeds as they moved. That meant they covered more ground faster. Hydrostatic transmission technology is used in many different machines today, including forklifts, harvesters, and construction equipment.

IH engineers had been testing hydrostatic tractors since the 1950s. They built the first hydrostatic tractor, the HD-340. Now the company wanted to take things up a notch! The Solar Aircraft team added a gas turbine engine to the HD-340 and renamed it the HT-340. The machine debuted in 1961 but never made it to production. It was a fun experiment, but the tractor guzzled fuel and sounded like a fighter jet when it started.

During the Space Age, IH had big ideas for what the future would look like. Here's one vision from 1970 where engineers are testing an engine. *Case IH*

In 1965, the Solar Aircraft division used its turbine knowledge to work on the **turbocharged** 1206 tractor. A turbocharged engine has a turbine wheel that pulls in air. With more air, the engine burns more fuel and makes more power.

Farmers had been demanding powerful two-wheel-drive machines. Other tractor companies made 100-horsepower two-wheel-drive tractors. These machines were stealing sales from IH. The bosses at IH told the engineers to "build 'em bigger."

The International 1206 was the engineers' answer. Released in 1965, it was the first IH two-wheel-drive tractor to break the 100-horsepower barrier. The tractor was an instant hit. Ten thousand units sold in its first two years.. The International 1206 blended two of Linda's favorite things: space-age engineering and tractors!

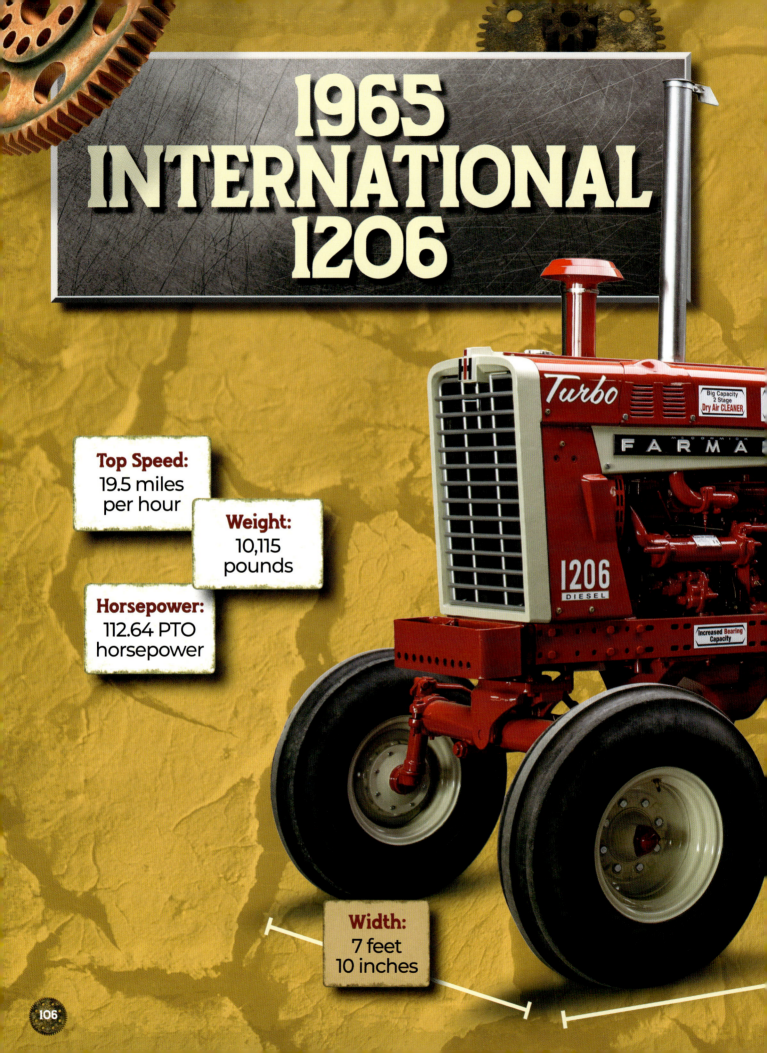

FUN FACT

The International 1206 was the first IH row-crop tractor to surpass 100 horsepower. This one is a rare prototype, restored with all the original advertising decals recreated!

Height: 7 feet 2 inches

Lee Klancher

Length: 12 feet 8 inches

1973 | HOWDY PARTNER!

Linda pulls her family's tractor into gear. Now she's married and has a four-year-old named Michael. Her husband, Dave, spends all his time on the farm. Linda is an engineer who designs assembly lines and factories. Even though she's an engineer, she still helps on the farm when she's not at work.

Linda looks at the muddy field. Will she be able to plow today, or will she just get stuck in the mud? Trying to tow a jammed tractor is a job she doesn't need. Worse yet, she could slide down the hill, or even flip the tractor over. If they had a four-wheel-drive tractor, she'd risk it.

The International 4100 was a rigid frame four-wheel-drive tractor. Companies now build the more flexible articulated tractors instead of rigid frames.
Wisconsin Historical Society 130933

Wisconsin Historical Society 129090

But it's not worth trying with their old tractor. Linda turns the engine off. She must wait until the field dries. Linda thinks about building a four-wheel-drive tractor from used parts. She's an engineer, after all! She was impressed by the ingenuity of the Steiger family and begins reading about their tractors.

When Steiger began selling four-wheel-drive tractors in the 1960s, IH scrambled to build its own. It quickly released the International 4300. The International 4300 had an impressive 300 horsepower, but it was too huge to do most farm jobs. IH only sold a handful. Then the company introduced the International 4100 tractor. The International 4100 sales were decent, but the tractor didn't take the four-wheel-drive world by storm. One reason may have been that farmers were attracted to articulated four-wheel drives instead of the 4100's rigid frame. Compared to rigid frames, articulated tractors turned more easily.

The builders of the International 4366 celebrate their achievement: building a sturdy, four-wheel-drive tractor in 110 days. Usually, tractors took years to develop.
Paul Nystuen Image Collection

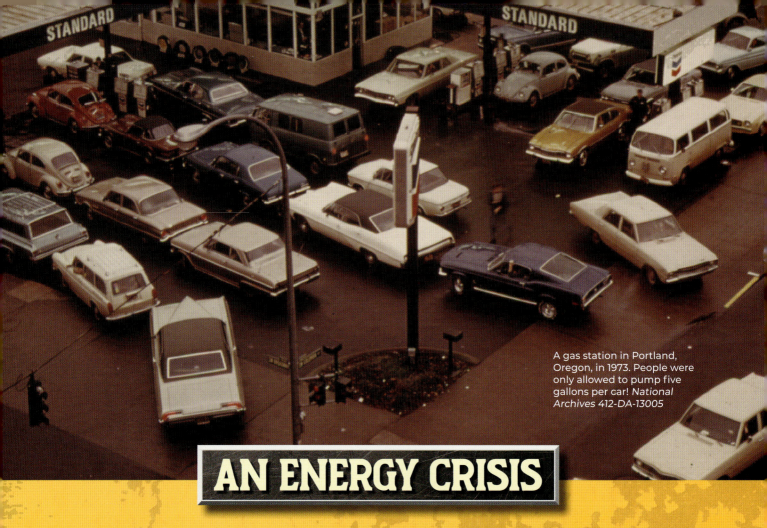

A gas station in Portland, Oregon, in 1973. People were only allowed to pump five gallons per car! *National Archives 412-DA-13005*

AN ENERGY CRISIS

In October 1973, oil-producing countries in the Middle East stopped shipping oil to the US. They did this to protest the US helping Israel in a war against Egypt. This caused an energy crisis. People stood in long lines to buy gas.

The energy crisis affected farmers too. At this point, most tractors ran off diesel fuel. In the past, many tractors were built with an "all-fuel engine." These machines could burn a variety of fuels, including gasoline or kerosene. But farmers shifted toward diesel in the 1950s and 1960s because diesel engines used less fuel for the power they created. The Middle Eastern countries began shipping oil again in March of 1974, but prices stayed high through the 1970s.

FARM FACT

Cesar Chavez

Migrant farmworkers move from farm to farm and work during the busiest seasons. Often, they face hardships such as low pay, no medical care, and no access to bathrooms. In 1962, a man named Cesar Chavez formed the Farmworkers Union. He persuaded workers to go on strike, or stop working, until their demands for better conditions were met. With the strikers, he marched 340 miles to Sacramento, California, to raise awareness of the problems facing farmworkers. The Farmworkers Union fought for and won higher wages and better treatment for its members.

IH looked at Steiger's success in building four-wheel-drive tractors. The small North Dakota company was beating IH in four-wheel-drive tractor sales. Instead of taking years to develop another new tractor, IH decided to work with Steiger. If you can't beat 'em, join 'em! Executives from the two companies spoke in 1972 about a partnership. IH agreed to buy 1,500 tractors over three years.

Steiger needed the partnership. Despite its success, it struggled to earn enough money to build tractors. Its factory in Fargo, North Dakota, had holes in the walls that let in freezing winter winds, and rabbits too! For the deal to work, Steiger had to do the impossible and move fast. Most tractors take years to develop. The International 4366 tractor was built in 110 days.

IH's partnership with Steiger allowed the small company to keep making their own tractors. *Scott Anderson Collection*

How did Steiger do it? The company sent its team of three engineers, including a college student, to a top-secret workshop in Fargo. The team worked nonstop until it had a **prototype**. It was exactly what IH wanted. The tractor combined parts from each company. It had an IH engine, axles, wheels, and paint. But the frame was Steiger's.

The International 4366 tractor was released in 1973. It marked the beginning of a happy partnership between the two companies. The market was growing too. Sales of four-wheel-drive tractors spiked from 2,728 in 1971 to 11,460 in 1975.

After the success of the International 4366, IH built more four-wheel-drive tractors with Steiger. With the cash, Steiger could finally move out of its rundown building. Soon, the company was making tractors in a brand-new factory.

After researching different tractors, Linda decides to buy an International 4366. She can't wait to drive it! The field is muddy, but she's ready to test it out. She turns the engine on, shifts into gear, and drives toward the crops.

CO-OP COUGAR II

FUN FACT

Steiger's partnership with IH wasn't their only one. The four-wheel-drive company built tractors for Ford, Allis-Chalmers, and Co-Op. The Co-Op Cougar II was a Steiger-built machine that was made for Co-Op Implements, a Canadian company. It is the same machine as the Steiger Cougar II, with different paint and decals.

Top Speed: 15.0 miles per hour

Horsepower: 227 horsepower

Weight: 22,000 pounds

Length: 20 feet 4 inches

Lee Klancher

1977 GOING FOR A SPIN: THE AXIAL-FLOW COMBINE

"Michael!" Linda shouts at her seven-year-old son. "Stay away from the combine!" Michael groans. What is he, five? He knows to keep a safe distance when the machine is running.

Linda and her husband have been spending the day harvesting. Now a corn stalk has jammed the machine. They must stop and clear out the stalk before they can work again.

Clearing a jam in a combine is dangerous work. Combines have many moving parts with teeth. Plenty of farmers have lost an arm or worse when they've tried to pull out a corn stalk out of a running combine. Linda turns the combine off and puts the parking brake on. They pull the corn out with a hard yank and start moving again.

Combine technology leaped ahead in the 1970s with the release of IH's Axial-Flow combine. This new technology spun the grain around a **rotary**. The Axial-Flow combine made farming even more efficient.

Engineers worked on the Axial-Flow combine in secret for years. Even higher-ups at the corporate office may not have known about the project! This International 1460 model was the first made. *Lee Klancher*

In 1974, IH tested the performance of the new combine against older models to see how well it worked. It passed the test! *Dave Gustafson / Case IH*

The idea of spinning grain to thresh it had been around since 1772. But no one had come up with a successful way to do it. In the past, IH engineers had designed a rotary corn sheller that worked well. A corn sheller separates corn kernels from the cob. Realizing they had something good, the engineers decided to build a harvester using similar technology.

In a secret garage, IH engineers started working on the new project. The team began in the late 1950s, thinking they'd need a few years to design the combine. In the end, the machine was released almost 20 years later!

Secrecy was important. Other companies could spy on the project and steal the technology for themselves. So, a small team of engineers worked inside a locked garage with frosted windows no one could see through. Almost no one knew about the secret project. The engineers tested all sorts of grain and crops to make sure the combine could work through everything. They also tested it in fields away from prying eyes.

Early on, the combine threshed corn easily. But it had issues with grain. The straw wrapped around the equipment and got stuck. But finally, the engineers had perfected the technology. The Axial-Flow combine ran faster and harvested more than any other combine. It was a leap ahead of the competition.

HOW AXIAL FLOW WORKS

Axial-Flow combines transformed harvesting. Traditional combines used slotted platforms that moved back and forth, separating the grain from the chaff. Some of them also used **threshing drums** that beat the grain against rasp bars. Rotary combines—like the Axial-Flow—separate the materials using a cylinder that rotates at high speed. The grain is flung out the side of the cylinder, and the chaff is sent out the back of the machine.

Rotary combines are much more efficient than traditional combines, meaning less of the grain stays on the chaff and is wasted. Rotary combines were very difficult and expensive to develop but much more efficient than traditional combines.

Parts of an Axial-Flow Combine:

Header: The header cuts the crops and feeds it into the combine.

Rotor cage: The grain falls through slots in the rotor cage.

Wisconsin Historical Society 114866

Rotor: The grain spins inside the rotor, giving it plenty of chances to separate from the rest of the plant.

Grain pan: As the grain pan swishes back and forth, the kernels fall through to the bottom.

Cleaning fan: The cleaning fan blows off any remaining pieces of chaff.

A rotor that has been removed from the combine.
Wisconsin Historical Society

A rotor cage inside the combine.
Wisconsin Historical Society

In 1977, there was a showcase of an IH combine against a John Deere combine. Despite the field being muddier than a pigsty, the Axial-Flow harvested the corn easily. And the John Deere? It got stuck in the mud!

Axial-Flow combines started rolling off the production line in 1978. They were so efficient that the rest of the combine companies were hard-pressed to catch up.

Michael hears his parents talk about the new IH combine. His mom is impressed by the engineering. The family buys one to help on the farm. They've been doing so well lately. Crop prices are up, and their family has been able to harvest more too! Life is good.

In 1978, IH introduced a rice-harvesting version of the International 1460. It had special features such as deeper treads on the tires for the muddy rice fields. *Wisconsin Historical Society*

1977 INTERNATIONAL 1460

Top Speed: 12.4 miles per hour

Weight: 26,190 pounds

Horsepower: 170.1 horsepower

Width (machine): 9 feet 2 inches

Width (header): 13 feet

FUN FACT

Developing the Axial-Flow combine took 50 years of engineering! The concept was invented early in the 1900s. IH engineers began work in the 1950s and spent more than 20 years perfecting their idea. The first Axial-Flow combine debuted in 1977.

Height: 11 feet 10 inches

Length (including header): 27 feet 3 inches

Wisconsin Historical Society 114866

A combine at work harvesting corn. *Lee Klancher*

CHAPTER 5 | 1979–1999

THE FEW FEED THE MANY

Eleven-year-old James yanks the tractor gearshift and moves it into gear. James already knows how to drive the tractor, but today, his parents have asked him to pull the grain cart. Once his father signals to him, he'll pull up to the combine so it can empty the harvested corn into the grain cart he's pulling.

Designed by Gregg Montgomery, Montgomery Design International

His father honks the horn. James moves the cart into place, but before he's finished, his father honks his horn three times. Oh no! That's the signal for unloading the grain. But James isn't in the right spot yet! If he's not there in time, the grain will fall onto the ground. James keeps his cool as he reverses the tractor. He makes it just in time to hear the kernels falling into the cart. That was a close one!

BY THE NUMBERS

Farms Become Supersized

Between 1900 and 1997, the number of farms dropped, but the average farm size grew. How did this affect farmers and their tractor needs?

Do you think tractors had to get bigger or smaller as the size of farms increased? Do you think tractors had to get more powerful or less powerful as farms got bigger? Why?

Use your imagination: What other tractor features would be helpful for farmers who spend more and more time in their tractors working as their farms get bigger and bigger? Can you list the features or draw them?

Year	Number of Farms	Acres per Farm
1900	5,737,372	146
1910	6,361,502	138
1920	6,448,343	148
1930	6,288,648	157
1940	6,096,799	174
1950	5,388,437	216
1959	3,710,503	303
1969	2,730,250	389
1982	2,240,976	440
1992	1,925,300	491
1997	1,911,859	487

Source: Census of Agriculture

Farm Income and Inflation

Between 1970 and 2000, the amount of money that farmers could keep in their pockets, in trillions, changed. In what year do you see the biggest change?

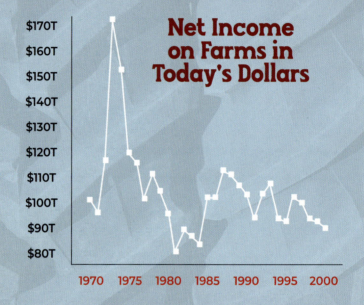

Net Income on Farms in Today's Dollars

Source: https://data.ers.usda.gov/reports.aspx?ID=17831#Pd8656e5ccf4f4a2dbf6b3b6bfc08c60e_2_105iT0R0x0

Farmer's Market

Between 1900 and 1997 the crops that farmers grew changed drastically. Here are a few examples. Which crop surprises you the most?

Crop	Percentage of Farms Growing This Crop in 1900	Percentage of Farms Growing This Crop in 1997
Corn	82%	23%
Hay and forage	62%	46%
Vegetables	61%	3%
Wheat	36%	13%
Cotton	25%	2%
Soybeans	0%	19%

Source: USDA-NASS

A tractor gets loaded onto a truck for delivery.
Case IH

It's 1981 and James's family has fallen on hard times. Many farming families have. The 1970s were so good that many farmers borrowed money from the bank to expand. They bought land and other equipment.

International Harvester Company (IH) spent a lot of money too—almost $1 billion—to develop new equipment. Things could've worked out if crop prices stayed high. But crop prices began to plummet. The US government banned selling grain to the Soviet Union, and farmers were stuck with a lot of crops and no one to buy them. Despite this, the price of fuel, **pesticides**, and other farming tools soared. The rise of prices is called **inflation**. Inflation can happen for many reasons, including a shortage of fuel and workers.

These challenges created the worst financial situation for farmers since the Great Depression in the 1930s. Farmers' debt reached higher and higher. Many struggled to keep their farms. Rural communities that once thrived started looking like ghost towns.

This was no time to buy new tractors. Farm equipment sales dropped 29 percent. IH didn't just face plummeting sales. The company lost $579 million when 35,000 factory workers stopped working for almost six months. In the last weeks of 1984, IH sold its farming division to a company named Tenneco. Tenneco also owned J. I. Case, and the combined company was called Case IH.

By 1988, things began to turn around. Congress had passed farming bills to help, and farms were becoming more profitable again.

A boy holds a sign at a demonstration in 1985. The 1980s were the hardest time for farmers since the Great Depression. *Wisconsin Historical Society 9267*

Even today, running a small farm is hard. This farmer saves money by using very old machines. Can you think of other ways to save money on a farm? *Lee Klancher*

FARMING THROUGH THE AGES

Wisconsin Historical Society 56753

1979 — A union strike at IH costs the company $579 million.

1979 — Tractorcade: Farmers drive tractors to Washington, DC, to fight for better farming policies.

1980 — IH builds the 2+2 row crop articulated tractor, which is nicknamed the Snoopy.

1981 — IH adds the Sentry System to its 50 Series. It's the first computer system on a tractor.

1982 — *Time* names the computer "Man of the Year."

1982 — Steiger offers a computer system on its Panther tractor.

Case IH

1984 — J. I. Case introduces a new line of 94 series four-wheel-drive tractors.

1985 — J. I. Case and IH form one brand: Case IH.

Case IH

Paul Natkin, courtesy of Farm Aid, Inc

1985 — At the peak of the farming crisis, Farm Aid hosts its first annual concert.

1986 — Steiger joins Case IH.

Case IH

1987 — Case IH debuts the Magnum tractor.

1997 — The Steiger Quadtrac tractor is introduced.

1979 | THE SNOOPY TRACTOR

James and his siblings are playing hide and seek on a Sunday afternoon. As his sister, Jennifer, counts to 100, he runs through the different hiding spots in his head. None of them seem tricky enough. But then James remembers the grain bin. They aren't allowed to go there, so Jennifer will never find him. As he scampers toward the bin, he hears an angry shout. "James! You better not be going where I think you're going," his father yells.

James doesn't understand. He knows every inch of this farm. Why can't he be trusted to be here too? James's father kneels and pats James on the back. "Your grandpa tried to unclog a grain bin. He fell in and couldn't breathe with the kernels crushing his chest. He died in minutes." James understands now. He'll be staying away from the grain bin for a long time.

James loves helping his parents on the farm. But today his father is in a bad mood. Their four-wheel-drive tractor does the heavy work, like plowing. But it can't cultivate. It's too hard to steer and the tractor's turns are too wide. James's dad can't hook any tools, like a mower, to the back either. The tractor has no power take-off to power the mower and other tools. They need a machine that moves over land like a four-wheel drive but is nimble enough to cultivate.

IH realized that farmers needed a four-wheel-drive tractor that felt like a two-wheel-drive. They wanted to build a brand-new tractor, but the company was low on cash. They had spent a lot on research and hadn't been able to sell enough equipment to make up the difference. To save money, they took the back of one tractor and combined it with the back of another.

An International 3588 in the field. These models were also dubbed "Snoopy" due to their oddly-shaped nose. Farmers often told IH dealers that the tractor was lighter, faster, and more manageable than their old two-wheel-drive tractors. *Oscar H. Will III Collection*

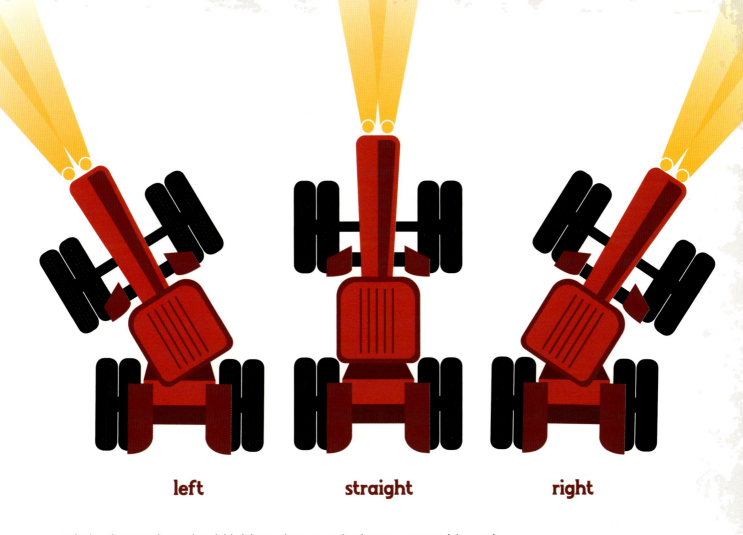

left **straight** **right**

Articulated tractors have a bendable joint so they can make sharper turns on tricky terrain.

The two parts were connected by an **articulation joint**. IH unveiled the 2+2 in 1978. The new tractor handled like a two-wheel drive but could do the work of a four-wheel drive. It also came with a rear power take-off.

Unlike many articulated four-wheel drives, the 2+2's **cab** was behind the joint. The cab is where the driver sits. This made for a funny-looking tractor with a long nose. The 2+2's look gave rise to plenty of names. The people at IH called it Snoopy since its long nose matched the comic strip character's snout. Others said it looked like an anteater. James's family called it the land shark.

Despite its appearance, James's dad takes the tractor for a test drive. He's worried that it will be hard to drive with that long nose, but the 2+2 handles well. Right now, times are tough for James's family, but they need a new tractor to grow more crops. James's parents end up buying the 2+2.

ROLLOVER PROTECTION

By the 1960s, it was clear that tractor rollovers were a risk to farmers. The three-point hitch had helped prevent backflips. Even still, hundreds of farmers died every year when their tractors toppled over. Without protection, the huge machines just crushed the drivers.

Starting in the 1960s, tractor makers offered ROPS—Rollover Protection Structures—as an option. These bars or cabs protect farmers from being crushed. Being budget-conscious, few farmers sprung for the extra cost. In 1986, tractor companies added ROPS to every tractor over 20 horsepower sold in the US. But even today, about half of tractors on farms don't have ROPS and about half of farming deaths are related to rollovers. Around 100 farmers die each year when their tractors overturn.

TRACTORCADE

In February of 1979, thousands of farmers descended upon Washington, DC. Many arrived on planes and buses. About a thousand drove into the capitol on tractors.

They were there to call attention to the growing farm crisis and to encourage the government to support the farming community. The value of land and crops was down, but the prices of diesel, seeds, and other farming needs were up.

Then a blizzard hit the city! The protesters owned some of the only machines that could move through the snow-covered streets. So, they helped dig the city out!

Unfortunately, the protests went unanswered, and the farm crisis only grew worse. The government didn't act until the mid-1980s.

Farmers drove their tractors to Washington, DC, to demand more action from the government. The tractors tied up traffic and blocked intersections. *Smithsonian Institution Archives, Acc. 11-009, Image No. 79-1712*

A button from the 1979 Tractorcade. *Division of Work and Industry, National Museum of American History, Smithsonian Institution*

FARM AID

Despite farmers calling attention to their struggles during the Tractorcade, times grew even more desperate in the 1980s. In 1985, a nonprofit called Farm Aid began to help farmers in need. It started a hotline where farmers could find useful resources as well as a fund to help farmers who had lost crops during floods and other disasters. To fund these programs, the organization hosted a concert with the biggest names at the time, including Willie Nelson, John Mellencamp, Bob Dylan, Tom Petty and the Hearbreakers, Bon Jovi, Billy Joel, Bonnie Raitt, and B. B. King. The benefit concert became an annual event.

Paul Natkin, courtesy of Farm Aid, Inc

No need to check your vision—this tractor is much smaller than the real thing! Engineers often build scale models of their designs to help them create and test new machines. This is a model of an International 7688, which was never produced.
Montgomery Design International

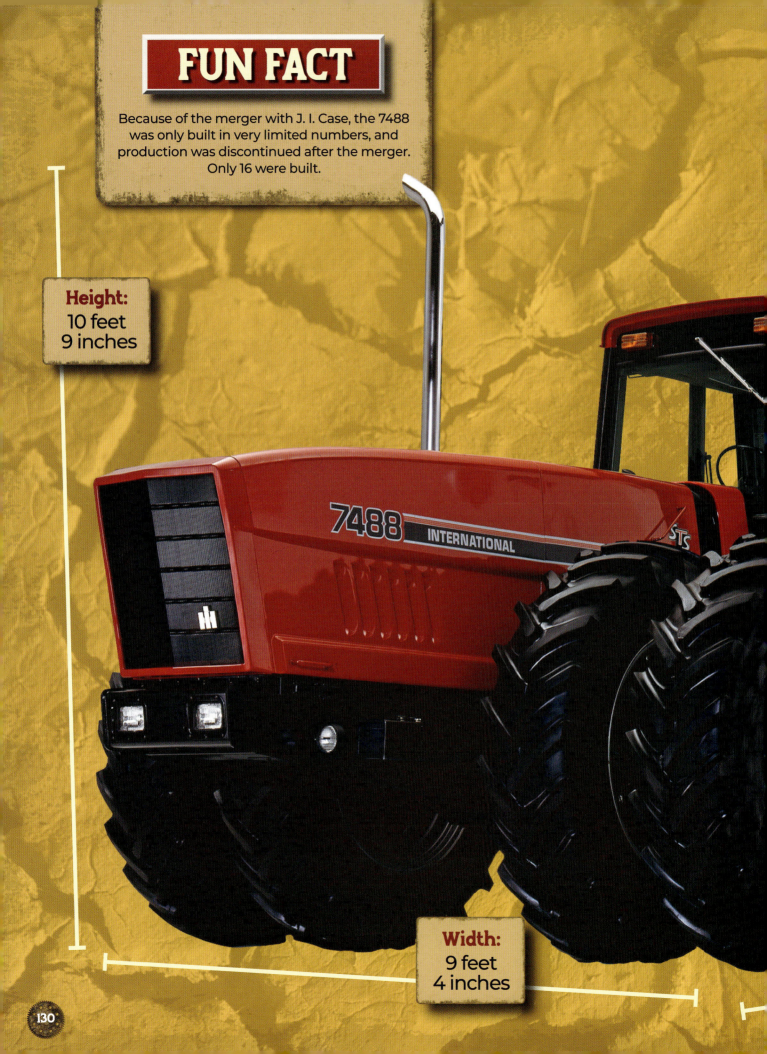

FUN FACT

Because of the merger with J. I. Case, the 7488 was only built in very limited numbers, and production was discontinued after the merger. Only 16 were built.

Height: 10 feet 9 inches

Width: 9 feet 4 inches

1984 INTERNATIONAL 7488

Top Speed:
19.1 miles per hour

Weight:
20,200 pounds

Horsepower:
235 PTO horsepower

Length:
19 feet 11 inches

Case IH

1982 DAWN OF COMPUTERS

The 1980s marked the beginning of the computer age. Even though people didn't have access to the internet yet, personal computers were becoming more available. The earliest ones were so huge they could fill an entire room . . . or even a house!

By the early 1980s, companies like Apple and IBM were selling personal computers that people could use at their home or office. They became so popular that *Time* magazine named the computer "Man of the Year" in 1982.

The Panther 1000 was Steiger's first tractor with computers. It came out in 1982. *Case IH*

An engineer designs the circuit board for the Steiger Panther 1000. Because it was the 1980s, engineers had to design every aspect of the cutting-edge computer system from scratch. Now, engineers can buy premade circuit boards. *Case IH*

James is now 12 years old and he's learning about computers in school. He has seen one and thinks they're the best! He can even play games on them! It's been a hard couple of years. James often hears his parents talking about money. They're worried that they'll lose the farm. His family can't afford a computer, but James hopes he can have one someday.

To help his family, James works on the farm more. He offers to give his dad a break from plowing. James's dad thanks him as the youngster climbs into the cab. Plowing the first row is easy, but then James looks down at the dashboard. The engine temperature is sky high! James groans and wonders what's wrong this time! The last thing they need is a broken-down tractor. He shuts the tractor off and waits for it to cool. James's dad returns, and the pair look at the tractor together. They're worried that the engine has been damaged. They don't have any extra money to spend on repairs. But it turns out that the screen protecting the radiator was caked with mud. The gunk kept the radiator from working properly. Once they clean the screen, the tractor runs smoothly.

IH was one of the first companies to add a computer to a farm tractor. The 50 Series came with the computerized Sentry system in 1981. The Sentry monitored the transmission to prevent damage and warn the operator if something wasn't right. That protected the tractor

COMPUTERS ENTER THE HOME

Percentage of Homes with a Computer

As the 1980s progressed, more families had a computer at home. The earliest personal computers looked very different from the ones we have today!

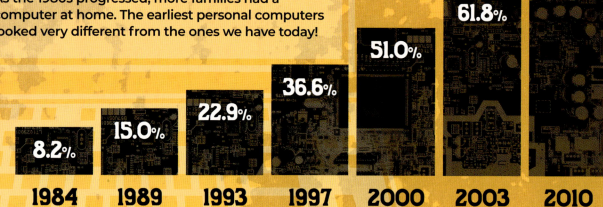

1984	1989	1993	1997	2000	2003	2010
8.2%	15.0%	22.9%	36.6%	51.0%	61.8%	77.0%

Library of Congress LC-DIG-gtfy-07166

ADDING POWER

The J. I. CASE 4890

At one time, J. I. Case built some of the biggest and most powerful four-wheel-drive tractors on the market.

Case IH

How do you add power to a tractor? There are many ways, including:

SIZE UP: Engines with larger pistons and cylinders can push more gas and air in.

TURBOCHARGE IT: Turbochargers push more air through the engine cylinders.

MULTICYLINDER ENGINES: Tractors originally came with one cylinder to power the driveshaft. But adding 4, 6, or 8 cylinders moves the driveshaft more quickly and smoothly. It also pushes more fuel and air through the system.

The 4890 was powered by a six-cylinder engine. Farmers liked six-cylinder engines because they had a reputation for being reliable and fuel efficient.

from getting damaged. If James's dad had a 50 Series tractor, maybe it wouldn't break down as much. Unfortunately, most farmers couldn't afford to buy a tractor with this new technology in 1981.

Like IH, Steiger moved into the computer age early. The company added a computer to the new Steiger Panther in 1982. The engineering team spent nights working on the system. They built the computer from the ground up and wrote all the software. The system helped shift gears when changing speeds. It also controlled the three-point hitch and the air conditioning system.

A salesman talks with a family about the International 3688 tractor. IH spent a lot of money in the 1970s and 1980s on research and technology. *Case IH*

1982 INTERNATIONAL 5288

Top Speed:
18.4 miles per hour

Weight:
14,610 pounds

Horsepower:
162.6 PTO horsepower

Width:
9 feet 4 inches

1988 | RIVALS UNITE: MAGNUM SERIES

James heads out early to the dairy barn to milk the cows. He leads them to the milking parlor and gets their feed ready. His sister, Jennifer, comes running and shouts his name. "You'll spook the cows!" he warns. But it's too late. The noise startles the cow he's hooking up and she kicks. Luckily, her hoof misses his sister's head by a few inches!

Now 18 years old, James wonders what he'll do when he finishes high school. He does well in his computer class. Maybe he could work on computerized farming equipment. But farming is dangerous. Look what can happen simply milking cows! Plus, farming is still looking grim. Some of the biggest companies couldn't make it during the **recession**. Even IH had gone under and been bought by another company.

In 1984, IH was in debt. A company called Tenneco bought IH's farming division. Tenneco already owned J. I. Case, so it combined J. I. Case and IH and called the new brand Case IH. The companies officially merged in 1985.

An early design sketch of the Magnum series from 1985. The Magnum combined the best of IH and J. I. Case. *Designed by Gregg Montgomery, Montgomery Design International*

The Magnum line set new standards for high-horsepower tractors worldwide. The brand-new diesel engine was small and quiet, yet powerful. It also had fewer parts and was easier to service. *Case IH*

When Tenneco first made the announcement to IH salespeople, it told them that Case IH tractors would come in a cream color. The IH dealers were so upset, they booed. They also wrote a letter to the head of Tenneco threatening to quit if the color was cream. They had red IH blood flowing in their veins!

Their reaction made an impression. Tenneco planned to show the cream tractors in Las Vegas in a week but decided to paint them red at the last minute. The team tasked with this job ran out of paint, with only a few days left to spare. They found IH red paint at a dealership in Casa Grande, Arizona, and put it on a **crop duster** airplane bound for Las Vegas. The red paint arrived in time, and the red tractors were met with a roar of approval.

Combining Case and IH was tricky. The two had been rivals for over a hundred years! How could people from these two companies work together? The best way was to build

THE PROBINE

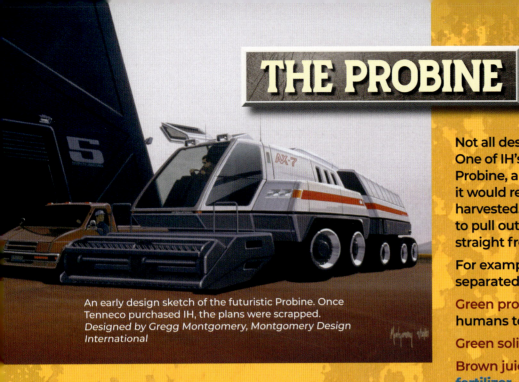

An early design sketch of the futuristic Probine. Once Tenneco purchased IH, the plans were scrapped. Designed by Gregg Montgomery, Montgomery Design International

Not all designs end up working out. One of IH's canceled projects was the Probine, a protein harvester. IH hoped it would revolutionize how crops were harvested. The Probine was designed to pull out protein from green crops straight from the field.

For example, alfalfa could be separated into three parts:

Green protein juice: For animals and humans to consume.

Green solids: Used as animal feed.

Brown juice: Sprayed onto the field as fertilizer.

The Probine project led to many futuristic designs and prototypes. There was even one idea to harvest seaweed in the ocean! But ultimately, the whole idea was scrapped when Tenneco bought IH's farming division.

What do you think a seaweed harvester would look like? Can you draw it or build it with blocks?

SOLVING A PROBLEM

Early Magnum tractors were high-performance machines. However, in a few situations, cotton farmers' Magnums caught on fire. The engineering team got to work. They needed to discover the cause of these fires.

They finally figured it out. Small bits of cotton often piled up on top of a heat shield. A heat shield is a barrier that keeps parts of a tractor from overheating. But they can still get hot. The heat shields would heat the stray cotton so much, it would catch fire.

Lee Klancher

To prevent the flares, the team switched the shape of the system from flat to curved. That way the cotton slid off the heat shield instead of piling up.

To help prevent flares and fires, engineers made a simple change that you can recreate:

1. Grab a piece of paper and, keeping it flat, see how many cotton balls you can pile on it.
2. Have someone bend (and hold) the paper in a rainbow-shaped curve. How many cotton balls stay on it now? More or less than when the paper was flat?

That's the same thing the engineers at Case IH did with this problem.

Can you come up with an even better way to solve this engineering problem? What shape would you use to keep cotton from piling up on the heat shield? Come up with some ideas and use paper or cardboard and cotton balls to experiment.

a new tractor! IH had spent years developing new technology. They had designed a new transmission and an upgraded cab. Many of the ideas hadn't become reality, though. IH couldn't afford it.

Now, many of these new features appeared on the brand-new Case IH series. The Magnum tractors made their debut in 1987. They were exactly what the doctor ordered. The new Magnums had a beautiful, modern look. They kept the IH signature red paint too. But most importantly, they drove well and were reliable. The engineers tested the machine for a total of 86,000 hours in the lab.

The tractor did more than bring better sales to the new Case IH company. It brought the two companies together. Both sides were proud of the Magnum series.

Spectators watch as the new Case IH Magnum is unveiled. *Cooper Hewitt Smithsonian Design Museum Archives.*

Height: 9 feet 10 inches

Length: 16 feet 7 inches

FUN FACT

The Magnum series appeared in 1987. This rare Case IH Magnum 7140 with front-wheel assist is the first of its kind that was sold.

1987 CASE IH MAGNUM 7140

Top Speed:
19.6 miles per hour

Horsepower:
197.5 PTO horsepower

Weight:
17,760 pounds

Width:
7 feet 11 inches

Lee Klancher

1997 | MAKING TRACKS

In the mid-1990s, farmers could finally breathe a sigh of relief. The recession was behind them. James is now grown up and works as a computer programmer. But in his free time he works his small farm. With the help of technology, James can still grow many crops in less time. Instead of spending a lot of money on a new tractor, James buys the old 2+2 from his family.

Today is mowing day. James hooks up the mower to the tractor. He starts mowing the front field, but bam! A rock flies and slams into the back window, cracking the glass. James is lucky the 2+2 has a cab. The rock could've hit him in the head! Even worse, he could've fallen off and gotten run over by the mower.

An early design of the Quadtrac. *Case IH*

Introducing the Magnatrac—an early Magnum fitted with tracks. *Case IH*

When James's parents sell the 2+2 to him, they buy a new Case IH Quadtrac. They tell their son that the ride is so smooth they can't even feel the ground. James's father planned to retire before he tested the Quadtrac, but because the machine is so comfortable he decided to keep working. James looks at his 2+2. He's happy with what he has right now. And maybe he'll be able to buy a Quadtrac in a few years!

The Quadtrac was many years in the making. In the late 1980s, Case IH began thinking about a tractor that had tracks instead of tires. With tracks, farmers could work in the wettest conditions that were usually unsuitable for tractors. The tracks almost floated above the ground. They also didn't pack the soil down as much as tires. This helped crops grow better. Caterpillar had released a tractor with tracks in 1987, and it was rumored that John Deere was building one too.

The engineering team designed and secretly tested the machine for years. They fit it onto a Steiger **chassis**. In 1987, Case IH purchased Steiger, the four-wheel-drive powerhouse, and added it to the brand. The addition made sense, especially since Steiger and IH had worked together in the past! The company unveiled red-painted Steiger tractors in August 1987.

Instead of two large tracks, the Case IH tractor had four tracks. This gave the machine better traction and made it more maneuverable. But the engineers struggled making tracks that could handle higher speeds of 20 miles per hour. They called in Goodyear, a tire company, to help them make the tracks. The new and improved tracks had cables that held everything together.

The first prototypes were tested in the middle of the night at a remote farm in the Midwest. Finally, they were ready to be revealed to the world. When the early models appeared at the Farm Progress Shows in 1993 and 1994, they were a hit. The Quadtrac finally hit the market in 1997. The result was a machine that could handle any kind of terrain and the worst field conditions. Today, the Quadtrac is one of Case IH's most popular machine lines.

This 2013 Steiger 620 Quadtrac has a more modern look! What are some of the differences you see? *Case IH*

FARM FACT

A Big Debate: Tracks Versus Wheels

After the Quadtrac's debut, many farmers switched from wheels to tracks. But even today farmers debate the pros and cons of each. Farmers must weigh their options and choose what works best for them. Here are some benefits of each.

Benefits of a Wheeled Tractor:
- Less expensive than tracks
- Less maintenance
- Better traction on pavement
- More fuel efficient
- Faster

Benefits of a Tracked Tractor:
- More pull than most wheels
- Can't go flat like tires
- Better traction on wet, muddy fields
- Doesn't create big ruts
- Smoother ride

The first Quadtracs were tested in secret and unveiled at the 1992 Farm Progress Show. Case IH hid the new machine in a hole in the ground covered by a small barn. People were amazed when the large tractor emerged! The Quadtrac was an instant hit. *Case IH*

1997 CASE IH QUADTRAC 9370

FUN FACT

Compared to two-track tractors, the Quadtrac's four tracks offer a smoother ride and have more traction when turning. Most modern-day tracked tractors use four tracks rather than two.

Wheelbase Length: 12 feet 4 inches

Top Speed: 18.7 miles per hour

Weight: 44,000 pounds

Horsepower: 315 PTO horsepower

Height: 11 feet 8 inches

Width: 10 feet

Lee Klancher

Machines from Case IH are ushering in a new era of farming where technology reigns. *Lee Klancher*

CHAPTER 6 | 2000–2020 AND BEYOND

COMPUTERS TRANSFORM FARMING

Twelve-year-old Hannah shouts after her friends as they open the door to the farm office. "You guys, we're not supposed to go in there!" But her friends laugh and keep going. Not wanting to look scared, Hannah finally follows the group. She groans when she sees her friends huddled around the computer.

"Let's play a game," one of her friends says. "Guys, really, this isn't that kind of computer," Hannah says. Her friend, Emily, closes the program that was on the computer. Hannah holds her breath. She hopes her dad saved his irrigation schedule before the program closed!

Case IH

BY THE NUMBERS

Feeding the World

Farmers have become more and more efficient at growing crops. How many more people can one farmer feed in 2022 versus in 1980? How about in 2022 versus 1820?

Average number of people one farmer could feed

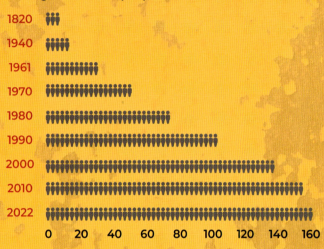

Sources: USDA 1962 Agricultural Statistics and Census p 432, Historical Statistics, p 469 https://www.census.gov/library/publications/1960/compendia/hist_stats_colonial-1957.html

Room to Spare

With modern technology and farming advancements, farmers have been able to get more out of one acre. The graph shows how much wheat a farmer could harvest from one acre between 1875 and 2017.

Compare this graph to the graph to the left, "Feeding the World." Do more bushels per acre make it easier for one farmer to feed more people? Why?

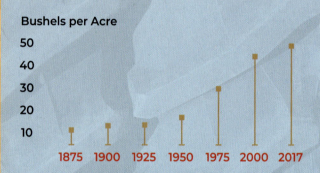

Source: https://www.ers.usda.gov/webdocs/publications/43783/39923_eib116.pdf

A Growing Country

The population of the US has boomed over the past 100 years. How did the farm population change during that time?

Year	US Population	US Farm Population
1920	10,790,000	111,271,341
1930	8,441,000	128,119,335
1940	7,589,000	138,601,511
1950	6,402,000	158,804,397
1960	4,531,000	186,720,570
1970	3,118,000	209,513,340
1980	3,275,000	229,476,360
1990	2,484,000	252,120,309
2000	2,392,000	281,710,914
2010	2,228,000	308,745,538
2020	2,600,000	331,449,281

Source: https://ourworldindata.org/employment-in-agriculture#number-of-people-working-in-agriculture
Source: https://ourworldindata.org/grapher/population-past-future?tab=chart&country=POL~USA~PRT~PYF

Combines unload grain that they just harvested. The combine transformed farm productivity. Modern combines can harvest about 25 acres of wheat in one hour! *Case IH*

It's 2006 and Hannah lives on a farm in Missouri. But her family's farm looks dramatically different than those from 200 years ago. Much of that is thanks to tractors. Farmers depend on technology rather than their hands to do much of the work, from planting to harvesting.

The age of the internet led to even more advances in farming. Today, computers and other technologies help farmers grow crops even more efficiently. **Satellites** circling the earth communicate with tractors and other farm machines to guide and make maps. Modern machines can put seeds in just the right place and add just the right amount of fertilizer at just the right time. Harvesters can map crop yields to change seed and fertilizer plans to make next year's plan even better. Scientific advancements have made stronger crop varieties and different ways to manage pests and weeds too. Farms can operate with fewer people thanks to these breakthroughs.

We'll need these breakthroughs and more for the future. By 2050, the earth's population is expected to reach almost 10 billion people. Plus, climate change may make it harder to grow crops. Farmers will need to use technology to feed the world in the face of droughts and extreme weather.

The next 200 years may bring even more changes than the previous 200. Today, scientists and engineers are studying how people can farm in space. We don't know exactly what the future might hold, but growing crops on distant planets may not be as far away as we think. The future is wide open.

This Quadtrac flies on a plane headed for Antarctica. It crossed 1,000 miles to the South Pole and hauled 250,000 pounds of cargo on the way! *Case IH*

Case IH has been building rugged machines to work in harsh climates for years, just like this Quadtrac. *Case IH*

FARMING THROUGH THE AGES

1983 — Korean Airlines Flight 007 is shot down, ushering in a new age of GPS.

1983 — President Reagan announces that once fully operational, GPS would be available for nonmilitary use. The GPS we know today was declared operational in 1995.

Satellites circling the earth. *National Archives 6364413*

1995 — Case IH introduces Advanced Farming Systems, which links GPS to farming information.

Case IH

2000 — The first crew of the International Space Station lives in space for four months, "turning on" the station.

NASA

2003 — Case IH reintroduces the Farmall tractor line.

2004 — Case IH launches the AFS AccuGuide Autoguidance System, which steers tractors in open fields.

2015 — For the first time, astronauts eat food grown in space—red romaine lettuce.

2016 — Case IH unveils its self-driving tractor.

CNH Industrial

2016 — The US government allows all farmers to use drones in their fields. Before, special permits were required.

Case IH

2017 — Case IH celebrates its 175th anniversary.

2020 — Case IH releases AFS Connect, a technology that allows farmers to remotely manage their farms, machines, and data.

Case IH

2021 — Farmers have more and more options for robotic weeders and fruit pickers.

ThisisEngineering RAEng

2005 | PERFECT CROP ROWS

Hannah hears her dad shouting her name from the barn. "Can you get out here?" he asks. "I need your help setting up the new combine." Hannah is thrilled to help her father. She is eleven years old and has a knack for computers and technology.

She runs into the barn to find her dad wildly pressing buttons on the family's new Axial-Flow AFX 8010 combine. "Why does everything have to be so complicated?" her dad grunts. Hannah grabs the manual from her dad and takes over.

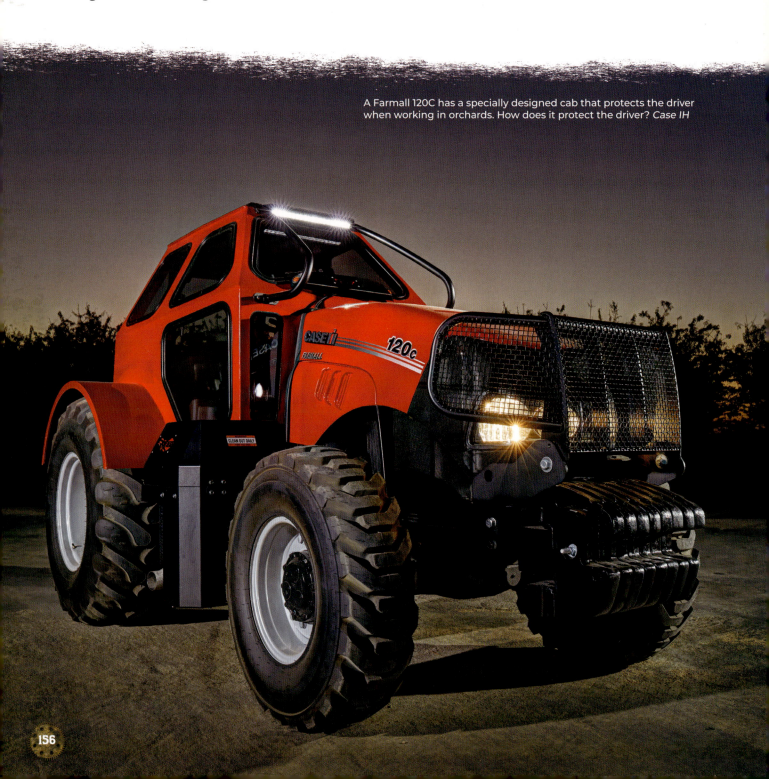

A Farmall 120C has a specially designed cab that protects the driver when working in orchards. How does it protect the driver? *Case IH*

For farms that are very large or have fields that are unusual shapes, combines like the Case IH 2566 can add guidance systems and more precise GPS receivers to help harvest more efficiently.
Case IH

It's a new age of farming. A whole host of technologies have emerged with the computer age. One of the most impactful is the **Global Positioning System (GPS)**, which became available to the public in the 1990s. GPS, is a tool that uses stations on Earth and satellites in space to pinpoint locations.

In 1983, Korean Air Lines Flight 007 unknowingly flew into the Soviet Union's airspace. The plane was shot down, killing all 269 people on board. As a result, President Ronald Reagan ordered the US Department of Defense to make GPS available to the public. Before, only the military could access the system. By 1995, there were 24 satellites in orbit, enough to give specific information for one's location.

FUTURE FARMING ENGINEERS

Elizabeth Jolly bought this 1942 Farmall H from her grandfather. The restoration took her more than 180 hours. *Lee Klancher*

Founded in 1995, the Delo Tractor Restoration Competition gives high school students the opportunity to restore a tractor and compete for prizes. The students research their tractor's history, restore the machine, and create a video about their experience.

One such machine was the International 1206. The 1206 arrived on the scene in 1965, with more than 110 PTO horsepower, making it a powerful machine then and now. Keaton Glass of Gonzales, Texas, restored an International 1206 for the competition. He's not new to restoring tractors—Keaton also restored a 1947 Farmall H that his grandfather had owned.

High school student Elizabeth Jolly from Pleasantville, Iowa, restored a 1942 Farmall H. She bought it from her grandfather, who had bought it in 2013 for $350 to save it from the junkyard. Jolly took it apart, checked and replaced some parts, and reassembled it. The tractor has never looked better.

Keaton Glass operates the powerful International 1206 that he restored. *Lee Klancher*

HOW CAN TRACTORS STEER THEMSELVES?

A Quadtrac working with auto steer in the field. See the little white box on top? That's part of the guidance system. *Lee Klancher*

Case IH has offered self-steering options for its tractors for years. But how does the technology work? There are three main steps to telling a tractor where to steer.

1. A GPS receiver on the roof tells the tractor its location. Farmers can choose GPS options that are accurate within an inch!
2. If a tractor is tilted on a hill, the GPS could be wrong. A system of **accelerometers** and **gyroscopes** measures the tractor's angle and motion and corrects the tractor's course.
3. The information is sent to the **steering valve**, which controls where the tractor goes, whether it's to the right, to the left, or straight.

In the 1990s, Case IH started adding GPS technology to its tractors. The first features were called the EZ-Guide and EZ-Guide Plus systems. The system's display showed farmers where they needed to steer to make perfect rows. In 2004, Case IH released an automatic steering system that got rid of the need to steer in open fields. It controlled the steering down the field. With both systems, drivers only need to grab the wheel at the end of each row. By 2015, more than one-third of US farmland was farmed using self-guidance systems!

Automatic steering has helped farmers in many ways. First, it prevents tractors from overlapping rows. Each part of the field gets the right amount of seed, fertilizer, and pesticides, which keeps costs down. Second, tire tracks stay on the same path and reduce soil **compaction**. Crops don't grow as well in compacted, or hardened, soil. Third, more accurate driving cuts down on fuel costs and wear and tear on the tractor. Finally, farmers have long days in the fields, so automatic steering gives the them a bit of a break. Hannah's family has the EZ-Guide system for their combine harvester. It helps them harvest their crops more efficiently and in super straight lines!

Look at that straight line! A Magnum 305 pulls a planter using a steering system that keeps tools from drifting from side to side. *Case IH*

2015 CASE IH AXIAL-FLOW 9240 COMBINE

Top Speed:
19.0 miles per hour

Weight:
42,205 pounds

Horsepower:
625 horsepower

Width of Header:
31 feet

Case IH

Height:
13 feet
4 inches

Wheelbase Length:
12 feet
5 inches

FUN FACT

This mammoth combine's grain tank can hold 410 bushels of grain, which is the same volume as 3,816 one-gallon milk jugs!

Combines like this one can now come equipped with precision farming systems that steer them and keep track of harvests.

2007 PRECISION FARMING

Thirteen-year-old Hannah hears her dad shouting, "We need to finish the harvest, now!" They've already delayed harvesting the soybeans for a few weeks because of rain. Wet soybeans get crushed by the combine and don't store as well. Plus, even though their combine can handle rough conditions, it's harder to cut wet plant stems. But Hannah's family can't wait any longer. There's a snowstorm coming in overnight. The snow could knock over the soybean crops and make the entire year a loss. Hannah runs out with her dad to hook up their four-wheel-drive Steiger 480 tractor to the grain cart. Her mom has already hopped into the combine and is moving it toward the fields.

They work all day, starting with the field that usually has the highest yields. Thankfully, they can manually change the combine settings to harvest the soybeans more gently. That way, the beans won't shatter during the threshing process. By the end of the day, they have covered about 75 percent of the entire farm. Technology helped them focus on the areas that grew more soybeans. Despite the weather, this year's harvest is as good as last year's!

Technology has made harvesting much more efficient. After the 1980s, when farmers were struggling to make money, farming management became very important. Farmers needed a new strategy for growing crops to increase their yields while spending less on seeds, fertilizer, and pesticides.

An early graphic shows all the Case IH machines that can connect to GPS. *Case IH*

Increasingly, they turned to **precision farming**. Precision farming uses GPS, data, satellite images, and computers to build a plan for farming precise locations in the fields. All the data combined tells farmers how much water, fertilizer, and pesticides to use. By understanding more about what's going into the crop, farmers can grow more in a smaller space. They can also use fewer pesticides and less fertilizer, which saves money and helps the environment.

Case IH was a pioneer of precision farming. It launched its Advanced Farming Systems in 1995. At first, the system displayed a map of crop yields on farms. The system calculated this by combining GPS data with how many bushels of grain the combine harvested. The map of yields

Advanced Farming Systems have progressed since it was first introduced. Now, with AFS Connect, farmers can log in from any device to see data about their machines and crops. *Case IH*

FARMING FOR THE FUTURE

Farmers are caretakers of the land. Many are working to make their farms more sustainable. Here are some ways that farms have done this:

Precision farming: Using technology to limit overuse of chemicals.

Soil conservation: Restricting tilling to prevent soil loss.

Cover crops: Growing different plants such as rye or clover to control weeds and insects, add nutrients without fertilizer, and keep soil from washing away.

Organic farming: Limiting chemicals.

A father and son look across their field. This farm may feed generations to come! *Case IH*

Farmers use technology to grow crops more sustainably. *Case IH*

Planting, harvesting, and other data can now be sent over cell phone networks from the machines in the field. *Case IH*

A farmer checks soil quality. Compared to the 1800s, today's farming tools look very different! *Case IH*

helped farmers understand their crops and plan for the next year. For example, if one section of a field did worse than expected, a farmer could adjust the amount of fertilizer used for next year. By the end of 1997, the team had a system that controlled applications of seeds and fertilizer.

The Advanced Farming Systems feature is still offered today. Year after year, it keeps track of how much fertilizer, seeds, and pesticides are used. The accuracy is within an inch! Based on how well the crops grow, the system makes changes to next season's farming plan. Today, Case IH also offers precision planting. The system remembers where it has planted seeds. If the tractor rolls over that area, parts of the planter shut off. This prevents double planting. Besides wasting seeds, double planting lowers yields because crowded plants don't grow as well as well-spaced plants.

Hannah's family uses Advanced Farming Systems. She loves keeping track of which new features are available each year. Someday, she hopes to help farmers set up precision planting systems.

2015 STEIGER 450

FUN FACT

Even though the lime green color has been swapped out for red, the Steiger brand continues to shine through.

Width: 10 feet

Top Speed: 21.1 miles per hour

Weight: 36,048 pounds

Horsepower: 451 PTO horsepower

Height: 12 feet 7 inches

Length: 24 feet 3 inches

Case IH

2016 | WHO'S AT THE WHEEL?

Twenty-two-year-old Hannah is home from college where she's studying to become an agricultural engineer. She's picking up rocks from the fields with her family. It's important to move them so they won't damage the farming equipment. Her young nieces and nephews make a race out of it to see who can pick up the most.

Hannah feels like she's herding cats. She shouts, "Stay behind the tractor!" She doesn't want the kids to get run over. Self-driving tractors Hannah just read about sure would make her life easier! Tractor companies are experimenting with machines that can drive themselves and stop when there's something in the way.

Case IH's Autonomous Concept Tractor works in the fields. After this prototype was displayed, Case IH incorporated a lot of its technology into its large models. *Case IH*

The Autonomous Concept Tractor is unveiled at the 2016 Farm Progress Show. It was a hit! *Lee Klancher*

Case IH began working on self-driving tractors in the mid-1990s. One of the engineering teams built a machine that was guided by GPS. It drove itself from the storage building to the test field. Once there, the tractor planted seeds then returned to the storage building. This early tractor hadn't reached the safety standards to be completely self-driving. Someone had to stay in the cab.

In 2016, Case IH revealed a self-driving tractor prototype. The **Autonomous** Concept Tractor had no cab. It could work alone on previously mapped routes or be directed by a regular tractor with a driver inside. The autonomous tractor had safety features that stopped or redirected the machine when it detected a vehicle, person, or other object in the way. It also stopped if it lost the GPS signal. That prevented a runaway tractor situation!

With self-driving tractors, machines could take advantage of good weather periods. Sometimes there might only be four or five days when the planting conditions are ideal. Self-driving tractors could work day and night during those short periods, unlike a human who needs sleep.

AUTONOMOUS TECHNOLOGY

The First Driverless Tractor

Radios were popular in American homes during the late 1920s and early 1930s. Families gathered around the radio to listen to music, stories, and the news.

But in 1932, J. J. Lynch used radio equipment for something completely different—to drive a tractor! Lynch steered a driverless tractor as it plowed a 30-acre field. Though this was an oddity, manufacturers are now building driverless, or autonomous, tractors.

An operator checks the wiring on the radio-controlled McCormick-Deering Farmall F-30 tractor in 1931. *Wisconsin Historical Society 25495*

Farms of the future? A farmer uses a tablet to drive an autonomous tractor. Photo 143879293 - ©Scharfsinn86 | Dreamstime.com

How a Driverless Car Sees

The technology on driverless cars is like that on tractors. They both use GPS to tell their location.

Here's how cars can see to drive themselves.

LIDAR UNIT
Constantly spinning, the lidar unit uses laser beams to generate a 360 degree image of the car's surroundings.

RADAR SENSORS
Uses radio waves to compute the distance from the car to objects in the road.

CAMERAS
Uses multiple viewpoints and angles from many images to find the distance to various objects. Cameras also detect traffic lights and signs, and help recognize moving objects like pedestrians and bicyclists.

MAIN COMPUTER (LOCATED IN TRUNK)
Analyzes the incoming data from the sensors to make driving decisions.

ADDITIONAL LIDAR SENSORS

In the future, self-driving tractors will be able to read weather forecasts to automatically take advantage of good conditions. For example, a tractor could stop during a rainstorm and then start working again once the field is dry.

As of 2022, Case IH's self-driving tractor is still an early prototype. It won't be on the market for a while. But many features from the self-driving tractor have made it onto available tractors. For example, some tractors automatically turn at the end of each row.

It's unclear how many farmers are excited about using a self-driving tractor. Technology has changed so fast that some remember the days where they steered their tractors down long rows of crops. But others might embrace a machine that helps them finish more work in less time.

Hannah is excited about self-driving tractors. Right now, she has a summer internship designing precision farming systems. When she graduates from college, she wants to help farmers set up autonomous systems on their land.

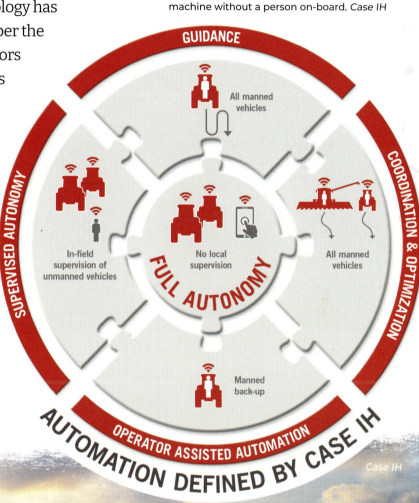

Automation of farm tasks can either assist an operator or—as shown in the center—run the machine without a person on-board. *Case IH*

Case IH

Equipment like this precision disk air drill can plant seeds with an accuracy that's within an inch! *Case IH*

FUN FACT

A Magnum like this one provided the base for the Autonomous Concept Vehicle.

2019 MAGNUM 380 CVX

Top Speed: 25.0 miles per hour

Weight: 32,300 pounds

Horsepower: 372.4 PTO horsepower

Length: 20 feet 7 inches

Case IH

THE FUTURE | FARMING IN SPACE

Hannah hears an alarm blaring. She is a Mars pioneer who volunteered to travel to the Red Planet as a settler. Her team lives in 3D-printed houses that were built by robots before they arrived. Solar panels power the entire colony. The solar grid usually works well, but right now a dust storm has covered the solar panels in a fine layer of grime. That means the solar panels won't get enough light to provide oxygen to the settlers or power the farming system.

Hannah deploys the cleaning team. Thankfully, they have trained for this. Soon enough, the team has scrubbed the panels. Hopefully, it'll be a while before the next dust storm!

Futuristic design for a Case IH electric tractor capable of working in harsh environments like space. *Designed by Gregg Montgomery, Montgomery Design International*

Case IH is always looking toward the future. This illustration from 1975 shows what a farm of the future might look like. *Designed by Gregg Montgomery, Montgomery Design International*

Does Hannah's future seem far-fetched? Well, yes and no. Today, NASA and other research institutions are studying how humans can live in space for long periods of time. That means growing food in space. Astronauts have already grown vegetables like lettuce, kale, and cabbage on the International Space Station. And scientists have learned a lot about how to farm in space, whether it's on a spaceship, Mars, or some faraway planet in another solar system.

There are many challenges to farming in space. Plants need a few key ingredients to grow. These are sunlight, water, nutrients, and a gas called **carbon dioxide**. Plants breathe in carbon dioxide to make food. Space doesn't provide these needs, so humans must design a solution.

For example, since Mars is farther away from the sun, the sunlight is weaker. So, researchers use lightbulbs called LEDs to help plants grow. On the International Space Station, different test farms emit the right kind of light to grow vegetables.

EMERGING TECHNOLOGY IN FARMING

Farming technology is changing at a fast pace. Here are some trends to watch for.

Drones: Farmers are beginning to use drones to keep an eye on their fields. The aircraft can fly over fields to make sure plants are growing well without stress from disease or insects. They can also act as crop dusters and treat crops with pesticides or fertilizers.

Robots: Automated farming is reaching a new level. Today, there's a robot that uses lasers to zap weeds on farms. Other weed-killing robots spray herbicide on invading plants. And companies are building robots that can identify and pick ripe fruit.

A farmer uses drone footage to gather important information about his field. *Case IH*

Do you do chores where you live? What kind of robot or drone would help you with your chores?

Sensors: Farmers increasingly use sensors that can detect moisture and fertilizer levels near plants. This information tells farmers when to fertilize and water their plants so they can use these resources more efficiently.

Different fuel sources: A tractor that runs on poop may not be so far-fetched. Tractor companies, including Case IH, are developing tractors that run on different fuels such as hydrogen and biofuels made from manure. They're also exploring electric tractors.

Robots are becoming more common on farms. This one roams through a corn field to collect information that will help farmers care for their crops more efficiently and breed better plants. The information includes the plants' sizes and the number of ears they grow. *EarthSense, Inc*

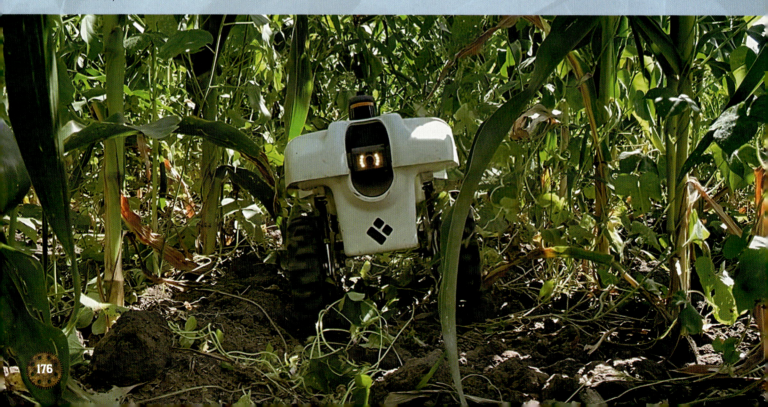

Plants tend to get nutrients from the soil. But Mars has no soil. It's only covered in a layer of crushed rock that holds some toxic chemicals. A type of farming called **vertical farming** takes away the need for soil. Vertical farms are indoor systems where crops are grown in towers. The water, lighting, air temperature, and nutrient sources are carefully controlled. Vertical farms are already growing crops on Earth. They may be the solution to getting plants what they need on the moon, Mars, and beyond.

Hannah's colony uses vertical farming to grow a small crop of fruit and vegetables. Most of the colony's food arrives on spaceships from Earth. Someday, they hope to expand the colony so they can grow all their food. Soon, small robots will pick strawberries and other crops. Another team of robots will clean solar panels!

Today, space farming seems like science fiction rather than science fact. But every day, researchers are learning more and more about how crops grow. The more we can understand about our planet, the better we can farm and feed the world . . . and beyond!

NASA ON EARTH

NASA may look to the planets and stars, but the space agency also has brought technology to Earth. Here are some of the ways NASA has helped farming.

GPS: In the 1990s, GPS could be off by as much as 30 feet. That's fine in most situations, but not when it comes to precision farming. NASA developed software to correct for GPS errors and make locations accurate to within inches.

Drought forecasts: NASA satellites can track drought conditions and help farmers manage water better. This information helps farmers change their watering methods and schedule planting to increase crop yields.

LED lights: LED lights use less energy while still helping plants grow. NASA space farming research has led to new lighting systems in greenhouses that help plants grow better.

Crop forecasts: Computers predict crop production for farmers using many factors, including drone images and NASA satellite data. This helps farmers plan for the future.

Space salad! Astronauts Scott Kelly (right) and Kjell Lindgren (left) nibble on the first food grown and harvested in space. *NASA*

NASA astronaut Michael Hopkins holds red romaine lettuce that was grown on the International Space Station with the help of LED lights. *NASA*

FUTURISTIC COMBINE

Horsepower:
Not much—it will be small!

Weight:
Very light!

Top Speed:
50-60 miles per hour

Size:
This combine will not need to carry an operator so it will be small!

FUN FACT

If farming switches to using automated tractors, they will run 24 hours a day and can be small and efficient. Combines like this one may be the harvester of the future! How does this compare to the McCormick Reaper?

Case IH

GLOSSARY

accelerometer: A device that measures the change in an object's movement.

articulated: Connected by a bendable joint.

articulation joint: A bendable connection.

assembly line: A way of building things that divides the job into many small steps.

autonomous: Self-driving, or having the ability to drive itself.

axles: Rods that connect the final drive to the wheels.

cab: A protective, enclosed area where the tractor driver sits.

carbon dioxide: A gas that plants use to make food.

cash crops: Plants that farmers grow to sell and earn money.

center of gravity: Place where an object's weight is the same on each side and all sides are in balance.

chaff: The outer layer of grain that can't be eaten.

chassis: An automobile's frame.

combine: A machine that reaps, threshes, and winnows grain.

compact: Small.

compaction: The process of being pressed down and hardened.

conservation: The protection and management of Earth's natural resources and the wildlife that depends on them.

crankshaft: The part of the engine that changes the up and down movement of the pistons into a turning, rotational movement.

crop duster: An airplane that sprays chemicals onto fields.

cultivation: Breaking up dirt around plants.

cylinders: Tube-shaped parts inside an engine.

differential: A group of gears that sends different amounts of power to the wheels.

disc harrow: A cutting machine that breaks up soil to prepare it for planting.

draft animals: Animals, such as horses, oxen, or mules, that can pull heavy loads.

drought: A period of above-normal dryness.

exhaust: The result of burning gas and air that's usually made of soot, carbon dioxide, and water.

fertilizer: A substance, like manure or a chemical mixture, that adds vital nutrients to help crops grow.

final drive: The last part of the gearbox that powers the wheels.

flail: A tool usually made of two sticks that helps with threshing.

four-wheel drive: A feature where all wheels receive power from the engine.

friction: The force that acts between two objects that rub or slide past each other.

fuel efficient: Needing less fuel compared to other machines in its class.

gangplows: Rows of plows.

Global Positioning System (GPS): A tool that uses stations on Earth and satellites in space to pinpoint locations.

grain cradle: A tool that cuts and gathers grain.

gyroscopes: Devices that measure angles.

harvest: To gather crops.

heat shield: A barrier that keeps parts of a tractor from overheating.

herbicides: Chemicals that kill weeds.

hydraulics: A way to power tools with the movement of water, gas, and other liquids.

hydrostatic: Powered by fluid.

implements: Tools.

inflation: The rise of prices.

internal combustion engine: An engine that is powered by explosions of fuel.

lobbied: Tried to convince people or governments.

lubricated: Oiled.

maneuverable: Easy to steer.

mower: A machine that cuts down grasses and plants.

pesticides: Chemicals that kill bugs.

piston: A sliding rod that moves up and down inside a cylinder.

planter: A machine that plants larger seeds, such as peas, in rows.

plows: Heavy tools that turn and loosen soil.

power: Source of energy.

power take-off (PTO): A feature that transfers power from a tractor to an attached tool.

precision farming: A kind of farming that uses GPS, data, satellite images, and computers to build a plan for farming precise locations in the fields.

prototype: An early test model of a machine.

radiator: A device that cools engines.

reap: To cut and gather crops.

recession: A slowdown of the economy and money.

revolutionized: Completely changed.

rotary: A turning tube.

steering valve: A device that controls whether a tractor turns or stays straight.

three-point hitch: A way to connect a tool to a tractor.

threshing: Separating grain from a plant.

threshing drum: A rotating cylinder inside a combine that beat the grain against rasp bars to separate it from the chaff

torque: A turning force.

traction: The ability of a tire to grip the ground.

traction engine: A steam-powered tractor.

tractor: A vehicle often used on farms that can haul heavy equipment.

transmission: A gearbox which sends power from the engine to the wheels.

turbine engines: Engines with spinning fan blades that suck in air.

turbocharged: Having a feature that pulls air into an engine, making it more powerful.

two-wheel drive: A feature where only the front or rear wheels receive power from the engine.

satellites: Objects that circle larger objects in space.

seed drill: A tool that plants smaller grains, such as wheat, in closely spaced rows.

sensors: Devices that can sense certain qualities, such as temperature or water content.

sustainable: Using resources in such a way that they will continue to be available in the future.

vertical farming: A type of indoor system where crops are grown in towers.

winnow: Clean by blowing air.

INDEX

acre, 19
Advanced Farming Systems, 155, 163–65
AFS AccuGuide Autoguidance System, 155
A. M. Archambault & Company, 4
Anderson, Jo, 6, 7
assembly lines, 49
Autonomous Concept Tractor, 168–71
autonomous farming technology, 176
Axial-Flow Combines, 95, 114–17
    AFX 8010, 156–57
    how axial flow works, 116
    9240, 160–61

Benjamin, Bert R., 65, 67
Boys Working Reserve, 53
Braceros, 81
bushel size, 19

Case IH
    beginnings of, 124
Case IH tractors
    AFX 8010 combine, 156–57
    Magnatrac, 145
    Magnum Series, 139–43
    Magnum 305, 159
    Magnum 380 CVX, 172–73
    Magnum 7140, 142-43
    Quadtrac, 144–49, 154
    Quadtrac, 9370QT, 148–49
    Axial-Flow 9240 combine, 160–61
Chavez, Cesar, 95, 110
Case, Jerome Increase. *See* J. I. Case
combine harvester, 16, 17, 80
    dangers of, 80
    futuristic design concept, 178–79
    See also Axial-Flow Combines; Moore, Hiram
Co-Op Cougar II, 112–13

Delo Tractor Restoration Competition, 158
Dust Bowl, 63, 72–75

energy crisis, 110
EZ-Guide system, 159
Farm Aid, 129
Farmall
    Cub, 85
    introduction of, 62, 64–67
    Letter Series, 63, 73
        A, 76–77
        C, 84, 85
        H, 59, 85, 87, 158
        M (Super M), 85, 88–89, 92
    Regular, 70–71, 92
    120C, 156
    460, 95
    560, 95
Farmerettes, 43
    See also Women's Land Army of America
Farmworkers Union, 110
featured tractors
    Co-Op Cougar II, 112–13
    Futuristic Combine, 178–79
    J. I. Case 150 HP, 26–27
    McCormick Reaper, 8–9
    1869 J. I. Case "Old No. 1," 14–15
    1908 International Friction-Drive Tractor, 38–39
    1915 McCormick No. 1 Harvester-Thresher, 20–21
    1918 International 8-16, 50–51
    1919 Mogul 10-20, 44–45
    1928 Farmall Regular, 70–71
    1928 McCormick-Deering 15-30, 56–57
    1944 Farmall A, 76–77
    1952 McCormick-Deering No. 127-SP, 82–83
    1954 Farmall Super M-TA, 88–89
    1965 International 1206, 106–107
    1968 Steiger 2200, 100–101
    1977 International 1460, 118–19
    1982 International 5288, 136–37
    1984 International 7488, 130–31

    1987 Case IH Magnum 7140, 142–43
    1997 Case IH Quadtrac 9370, 148–49
    2015 Case IH Axial-Flow 9240 Combine, 160–61
    2015 Steiger 450, 166–67
    2019 Magnum 380 CVX, 172–73
Ferguson, Harry, 63
final drive, 99
foreclosure auctions, 74–75
    See also Dust Bowl
Fordson, 46–47
four-wheel drive, 97–98
Froelich, John, 33, 34–35

Global Positioning System (GPS), 155, 157–71, 177
grain binders, 16–18
Great Depression, 62, 63, 72–73
The Homestead Act, 2, 3, 10
The Horse Association of America, 61–63
horsepower, 19
hydraulic power, 104
hydrostatic transmission, 103–5

IH tractors
    Friction-Drive tractor, 33, 38–39, 92
    HT-340, 103, 105
    Mogul 8-16, 40, 41
    Mogul 10-20, 41, 44–45
    Titan 10-20, 41–42
    Titan 15-30, 41
    Titan 45, 35
    2+2, 127
    8-16, 33, 34, 47–48, 50–51, 97
    15-30, 28
    454, 94
    660, 93
    1206, 105, 106–7, 158
    1460, 118–19
    3688, 135
    4100, 109
    4300, 91, 109
    4366, 109, 111
    5288, 136–37
    7488, 130–31
internal combustion engine, 32, 33
    how it works, 37

International Harvester Company
    creation of, 32, 33
    sale to Tenneco and creation of Case IH, 124, 138–41
    Solar Division, 102–3

J. I. Case, 4, 12, 33
J. I. Case tractors
    Old No. 1, 4, 12, 14–15
    65 Steam Tractor, 92
    150 HP, 22, 23, 25–27
    4890, 134

Loewy, Raymond, 73, 76, 87

McCormick-Deering tractors
    No. 123-SP, 80
    No. 127-SP, 82–83
    10-20, 33, 53
    15-30, 53–54, 56–57
McCormick Harvesting Machine Company, 6
McCormick tractors
    McCormick Reaper, 8–9
    No. 1 Harvester-Thresher, 20–21
McCormick, Cyrus, 4, 6, 8
Moore, Hiram, 4, 17

oil, function of, 43
Otto, Nicholas, 33

power take-off (PTO), 48, 55
precision farming, 162–63
Probine, 140

Quadtracs. *See under* Case IH tractors;
    See Steiger: Quadtrac

reapers, 6–9
Rollover Protection Structures (ROPS), 126

self-driving tractors. *See* Autonomous Concept Tractor
Sentry System, 125, 133, 136
Solar Aircraft. *See* International Harvester Company: Solar Division
space farming, 174–79

Space Race, 102–5
steam engine
    dangers of, 23–24, 31, 34
    how it works, 13
    See also J. I. Case tractors: Old No. 1
steam-powered tractors, 22–23
Steiger
    Panther 1000, 132–33
    partnership with IH, 111
    purchased by Case IH, 146
    Quadtrac, 125
    red, white, and blue tractor, 90
    #1, 92, 95, 96
    450, 167
    480, 162
    2200, 100–101

threshers, 10–12
    See also J. I. Case tractors: Old No. 1
three-point hitch, 63, 85–87, 128
Tractorcade, 125, 128–29
Tractorettes, 79
    See also Women's Land Army of America
transmissions, 81
turbine engines, 103

vertical farming, 177

Whitney, Eli, 4
Women's Land Army of America, 43, 79
World War I, 40–43
World War II, 78–81

Illustration Credits

Envato*
    Close Up Metal Rot Texture Background, used throughout
    Gears silos, used throughout
        Aged Copper Spur Gear
        Clock Gears
        Dirty Clock Gears
        Dirty Silver Gear
        Rusty Gears
        Vintage Gear
    Manual Transmission, 81
    Metal Plate, used throughout and on the cover
    Police Car Light, 170
    Tractor Tires/Wheels Closeup Pattern, used throughout
    Vintage Open-Closed Sign, used throughout
    4x4 Chassis, 98

Pexels.com
    Wheat Close-Up, 3, 30, 60

PublicDomainPictures.net
    Computer Circuit Board, 134

PublicDomainVectors.org
    Apple Glossy, 19
    Car Accident, 30
    Corn Logo, 19, 48
    Football Gridiron, 19
    Hay in Cart, 19
    Johnny Automatic Horse Silhouette, 19
    Lightning Icon, 30
    Milk Containers, 19
    Pig Silhouette, 48
    Portable Steam Engine, 13

Sports Car BW, 19
Stick Figure, 92
Stylized Computer, 134
Telephone, 30
Tractor, 60
Tractor Vector 2, 92
USA States, 3
Wheat, 19, 48

*Images in the Envato list above were downloaded by timpalincreative.com and sublicensed to Octane Press for the purposes of printing in *Revolutionary Red Tractors*.

Library of Congress LC-DIG-fsa-8d35974